6

# JACK RUSSELL
## AND
## HIS TERRIERS

# JACK RUSSELL
## TERRIER CLUB of GREAT BRITAIN

# JACK RUSSELL
# AND HIS
# TERRIERS

"DAN RUSSELL"

J. A. ALLEN
LONDON

British Library Cataloguing in Publication Data

Russell, Dan
    Jack Russell and his terriers
    1. Jack Russell terrier – History
    I. Title
    636.7'55          SF429.J27

ISBN  0-85131-276-4

Published in 1979 by J. A. Allen & Company Limited,
1, Lower Grosvenor Place, Buckingham Palace Road,
London, SW1W 0EL
and at
Sporting Book Center, Inc.,
Canaan,
New York 12029,
United States of America.
Reprinted for the Jack Russell Terrier Club of Great Britain 1999

Printed in Hong Kong by
Dah Hua Printing Press Co., Ltd
Trowbridge and Esher

# CONTENTS

## LIST OF ILLUSTRATIONS

# FOREWORD

The working Jack Russell is without doubt a canine superstar. This gallant little dog has so many attributes that make it what it is and what it stands for – a devoted and trusting friend with a character unsurpassed in the animal kingdom, equally at home as a fireside companion or at work all day on a hillside in the worst of British weather. It has the heart of a lion and is blessed with more intelligence, stamina, tenacity and versatility than any other breed of similar size and proportion. Developed and preserved for over 200 years by working terrier enthusiasts, this true-to-type white-bodied terrier, known and recognised throughout the world as the 'Jack Russell' is accepted as having a mixed and varied ancestry and owes as much to geographical location (within the UK) as it does to individual tastes and requirements for work.

The Jack Russell Terrier Club of Great Britain was formed in 1974 by a small group of working terrier enthusiasts to promote, preserve and protect the true working Jack Russell and to ensure it does not go the way of many of our traditional working breeds which are now a far cry from their honourable ancestors. From this humble beginning the Jack Russell Terrier Club of Great Britain has grown into an international organisation with affiliated clubs and regions totalling 12000 members worldwide. The club organises and enjoys, with fellow members, terrier shows and social gatherings and continues to assist and educate new members in the ownership, breeding and preservation of these remarkable little dogs.

Today the true working Jack Russell faces greater threats than at any other time in its history. This brave little terrier, much admired and revered for its courage, intelligence and loyalty, has had its reputation sullied by those who would seek to ban all forms of hunting, a ban which would not only destroy a unique part of our heritage but also bring about the subsequent loss of a truly remarkable little dog which has deservedly received international acclaim.

To celebrate the club's 25th anniversary the publishers have kindly agreed to republish this excellent book on the Reverend John Russell and his terriers and thus help to preserve both the book and the memory of the man to whom we and our terriers owe so much. We are indebted to Dan Russell for his work in producing such a wealth of information and history on the life of John Russell and his hunting and which will always, I'm sure, be treasured by all Jack Russell terrier owners.

Our terriers are our pride and our heritage and we will continue our fight to preserve them. You too can help preserve this wonderful and unique superstar by joining The Jack Russell Terrier Club of Great Britain and supporting all our efforts on behalf of the working Jack Russell as we know it today.

Brian Male
Chairman JRTCGB
January 1999

# PART ONE

# JACK RUSSELL

# I

## INTRODUCTION

It was April, 1883. The churchyard of the parish church at Swymbridge in North Devon was packed with more than a thousand people, most of them in some sort of mourning. The interior of the church was filled with members of the great county families, the Mayor and Town Clerk of Barnstaple, representatives of the Freemasons, of the North Devon infirmary and many more. There were also twenty-nine clergymen. Outside stood country people from all around, most of them clutching little bunches of flowers.

They had come to say their last farewell to a man who was loved and respected throughout the West Country. He was no great county magnate, but a simple country clergyman who had worked among them for more than fifty years. His name was John Russell.

As the coffin was lowered into the grave, to lie beside that of his wife, little children, weeping as they went, filed past the grave, dropping into it little bunches of wild flowers, while at the head of the mound of wreaths was one from the Prince and Princess of Wales. They both knew how much John Russell had loved the Devon countryside and their wreath was composed of cottage flowers.

Although Russell was — according to his lights — a good parish priest, it was not because of his ministry that he was known so far and wide; it was because of his skill and endurance in the hunting field and because he was the protagonist of the type of working terrier which bears his

*11*

name to this day. His endurance in the saddle was phenomenal and the distances he rode in pursuit of his favourite sport seem almost incredible in this effete age.

It is scarcely more than a long lifetime since John Russell died, yet already the mists are closing in. Because of his Mastership of his own little pack of hounds and because he spent so much time in the hunting field he has been described as "completely worthless". Many of the stories about him have been handed down by word of mouth and, because such stories tend to become distorted in the telling, Russell has often become confused with two other clergymen who were quite unfitted to be in Holy Orders. They were the Rev. John Froude of Knowstone and the Rev. Jack Radford of Lapford.

Both of these men were contemporaries of Russell and were both known as "Jack". Russell knew Froude and was friendly with him and so, over the years, some people have tarred him with the same brush. In addition, he became so well-known for his sporting activities — and "Jack" being the popular diminutive of "John" — that John Russell was soon spoken of as "old Jack Russell", though seldom to his face. Hence the name of the breed of terrier with which his name is forever linked.

It has also been said that Russell dissipated his wife's fortune. It is true that, all his life, he suffered severely from lack of money and that his wife's money did enable him to keep hounds; but her fortune was far less than has been supposed and, as she too loved hunting, she was only too happy to keep the hounds going. The estate of Colleton was left to her sister, so the assertion that Russell was guilty of ruining it is quite untrue. Mrs. Russell's granddaughter, Miss Mary Russell, always stoutly asserted that her grandmother loved hunting so much that she was delighted to help with the upkeep of the hounds.

The file copies of the local newspapers of the time were mostly destroyed in the bombing of Exeter during the 1939-45 war, but there are two sources to which one can turn for the story of Russell's life. The first is the biography, *A Memoir of the Rev. John Russell*, by the Rev. E. W. L. Davies who was at one time Russell's curate and who became a lifelong friend. Davies was a great sportsman and earned the nickname of "Otter" when he kept a pack of otterhounds in South Devon. He coxed the Oxford boat in the first University Boat Race of 1829. After a curacy at Kingsbridge, where he kept his otterhounds, he went to Swymbridge and then to Buckinghamshire and Yorkshire, but in middle life he became paralysed from the waist down and retired to Bath, where he spent the rest of his life in a wheel chair.

Davies's biography does not reveal the whole truth about Russell because it was written towards the end of Russell's life and he corrected the proofs for accuracy, so that it stands to reason that anything he did not like would have been struck out. The picture that emerged is of near perfection and no one could have been such a paragon.

The second main source is *Hunting Parson* by Mrs. Eleanor Kerr, who gives a much more rounded picture of the man. It is clear that Mrs. Kerr has great sympathy with Russell, but she reveals certain imperfections of character which are far more true to life than the idealised portrait by Davies.

In addition to these two biographies, there are some of us who, many years ago, knew aged men who had hunted with Russell and from them we got a little first-hand information. Over the years the tales have been told and the legend has grown and it is more than likely that many of the stories are apochryphal, so that it is difficult to sort the grain from the chaff.

A. G. Bradley in *Exmoor Memories* describes how, as a

*13*

boy, he was crammed by the rector of Challacombe. One morning they heard a hunting horn, and looking out of the window, he saw Russell and his hounds. He describes him as a very attractive big man, riding some fifteen stone, a well set-up, clean-built old fellow in tall hat, black cutaway coat, tight breeches and boots looking the very picture of an old time sportsman.

At the present day, Russell would speedily have been in trouble with his Bishop for hunting too much, but it must always be remembered that he was the product of an age when hunting was accounted to be no sin. But Russell did have several differences of opinion with Henry Philpotts, his Bishop, to whom hunting was anathema. Out of these brushes it was Russell who invariably came off best.

According to his lights, Russell was a good parish priest. It is true that he did not visit his flock regularly, but the villagers did not expect him to because in those days there was a great gulf between the village folk and the upper classes. All that was expected was that the parson should be at hand in case of illness or trouble in a family. That is how Russell ran his parish. He spent a lot of time hunting but, if there were illness in a family, he, Mrs. Russell, or the curate would call without delay. After his death an old parishioner said "He may not have been all that of a parson, but he was such a man to make peace in a parish". Not a bad epitaph, one may think.

Peering back through the years we see a man of no great vocation and no particular intellectual attainment but who, nevertheless, won great renown as an eloquent preacher and who was always ready to give his services in a good cause; a simple man who did his duty as he saw it and whose religion was very real to him. There are, however, hints of intolerance and imperiousness; traits which can be found in many Masters of Hounds at the present time. He was also an hospitable man, but his natural generosity was sadly curtailed by his life-long lack of funds.

By middle life Russell had come to be regarded as a "character" and there can be no doubt that he was very proud of it. Almost up to his death at the age of eighty-eight, he continued to hunt and to ride prodigious distances, and one cannot help thinking that vanity and jealousy of his reputation caused him to do so on many occasions.

He left as his permanent memorial the type of working terriers which bear his name; so long as there are men who love a game terrier, the name of John Russell will not be forgotten.

## II

## YOUTH

John Russell was born on December 21st, 1795. He came of a family which had been in Devon since 1549, when Lord John Russell came to the West Country to suppress the prayer-book riots. John's father had taken Holy Orders and at the time of the boy's birth he lived at Belmont House, Dartmouth. When the young John was fourteen months old, his father moved to South Hill Rectory, near Callingham, in Cornwall.

It was here that the boy noticed that the Rector took a great part in the affairs of the village. The illiterate villagers would come to the rectory to ask the Rector to write a letter for them, or for help in time of illness. The parson was more easily available than the squire or landowner, but such was the class gulf between rectory and cottage that the villagers did not expect or want the parson to visit them in their own homes, except in case of trouble.

It was the observation of this state of affairs during his formative years that later set the stamp on John Russell's conduct of his parochial duties.

The boy's first school was Plympton Grammar School, at which Sir Joshua Reynolds had been a former pupil. It was here that John first encountered John Crocker Bulteel who later became his firm friend; but at this time young Bulteel was a bully and John soon fell foul of him. Some of the smaller boys told John that Bulteel had made some rude remarks about him, whereupon John tore up one of Bulteel's

Photographs of John Russell are few. This one was taken when he was eighty years of age.

A really lovely pair of terriers who not only win at shows, but also work regularly with the Braes of Derwent Hunt. They are owned by Mr. D. Hume of Consett, County Durham.

school books. He told Bulteel he had done it and that led to a fight. It was a bitter contest and John had the better of it and from then on there was less bullying by Bulteel.

John Russell's father accepted the offer of a curacy at Crediton. He was often absent on a day's hunting, but it is said that he was conscientious and "particularly tactful with dissenters". In order to eke out his meagre stipend he took pupils and hard work would be rewarded with a day's hunting for the pupil concerned. One of his pupils said that old Mr. Russell was one of the best classical scholars, one of the best preachers and readers and one of the boldest hunters in the County of Devon. He added that not infrequently he had seen the old gentleman's top boots peeping out from under his cassock.

Like many another incumbent of the day, Mr. Russell came up against the Bishop, Henry Philpotts, who was an extremely difficult gentleman to deal with. Philpotts had an almost insane love of litigation and was guilty of nepotism, as he made his son Archdeacon of Truro, which was the plum job of the diocese. During the cholera epidemic in Exeter in the 1840s he left the city and went to live in South Devon and was to have many skirmishes later with Russell's son, John. Philpotts clung on to office almost until his death at ninety-one, but in his later years he was not seen in the diocese as he preferred to live in his own house near Torquay.

One of the canons of the church laid down that no clergyman should cast out devils without the direction and licence of his Bishop. One of Mr. Russell's parishioners had the delusion that he was a cider-press and used to spin round, uttering a shrill squeak like a cider-press in operation. Mr. Russell prayed for this man in church, but the Bishop jealously assumed that his authority had been flouted and speedily reminded Mr. Russell of the canon forbidding the casting out of devils. There, fortunately for the Rector, the matter was allowed to drop.

After the move to Crediton, John Russell left Plympton Grammar School and was sent to Blundell's at Tiverton, which was then a depressed little town which had suffered much from the decline in the wool trade.

Blundell's, the great public school of the West Country, has long since moved to modern and bigger buildings, but the old school still remains much as it was in Russell's time. It was long and low with a dome rising above the roof. The walls are defaced with the names of former pupils cut into the stone.

It was fortunate for the young John that nature had endowed him with natural toughness, for boarding-school life in the early nineteenth century was anything but pleasant. The food was disgracefully bad. For breakfast each boy had one roll and a cupful of milk and water. An old woman carved the meat for the main meal and she was not too particular about the cleanliness of her hands. The meat was often high and the knives and forks were broken, some forks having only one prong.

The headmaster, Dr. Williams Richards, was typical of his day. He believed that boys could be taught only by knocking it into them and he often began the day with a flogging. In class he was fond of cuffing the boys round the ears. In later years, Russell said that, although when at Oxford he had set-to with some of the best men in England, he had never met a man who could hit as hard as William Richards.

The school buildings were in a terrible state; the roof leaked so that the rain blew in and dripped on the boys' work. In cold weather the ink froze in the pots, for there was no fire. There were, of course, no bathrooms; in the mornings, no matter how cold the weather, John Russell and the other boys washed under a pump in the yard. The wonder is that any of them survived to manhood.

In common with other public schools, there was a great deal of bullying. Very often junior boys were thrown into Taunton Pool. This was known as "sheep-washing". Another brutal practice was to hold a boy close in front of a fire, but this was prohibited after one boy died from burns.

From today's standpoint it seems odd that little attempt was made by the ushers to stop this bullying. The answer probably is that they were so ill-paid that they could not be bothered.

Young Russell was a tough little boy and it was not long before he crossed swords with one of the worst bullies, a monitor. A very difficult fellow for a junior to deal with.

It was some time before the opportunity came. Many of the boys were keeping rabbits, although this was against the rules of the school. This came to the headmaster's ears and he ordered that all rabbits should be disposed of immediately. Hunter, the monitor, had some rabbits and he decided to keep them until he could ask the headmaster's permission to send them home. Russell knew about this and he put one of his ferrets into each of the rabbit hutches.

When Hunter discovered the death of his pets he went to the headmaster in tears. The truth came out and Russell was summoned to the study. There Richards flogged him with a whalebone riding whip until the end of the whip was in splinters.

Because of the ban upon pets, Russell had to give up his ferrets, but it was not long before he had embarked upon another illicit venture. During his half-holidays he and a friend had been ferreting on local farms and had made friends with the farmers. They got the idea of keeping a few hounds.

Somehow or other they managed to get hold of four and a

half couple of old hounds and they kennelled them near the school with a friendly blacksmith. The boys' farmer friends were of a sporting bent and were only too glad to help keep the little pack supplied with flesh.

Of course, it could not last and some busybody who signed himself "Friend of Good Discipline" wrote to Richards — the cat was out of the bag. There was a fearful row and Russell was nearly expelled.

The fear of expulsion must have frightened Russell for he applied himself to work and came back into the headmaster's favour by winning an exhibition for thirty pounds, tenable for four years. To this he added a medal for elocution.

Heaven alone knows what William Richards would have said and done if he had known that Russell spent the first instalment of his exhibition on buying a horse. He would, however, have been delighted to hear that the boy had been swindled in the deal by the Rev. John Froude.

It was about this time that Russell had his first day's staghunting. He had lost hounds and was alone on the heather when a stranger came up and spoke to him. With the stranger's guidance Russell was in at the kill near Slade Bridge. His mentor was Dr. William Palk Collyns, author of the first, and probably the best, book about deer-hunting on Exmoor, *The Chase of the Wild Red Deer*.

From that day Russell hunted with the staghounds for nearly seventy years. Many years later, as an old man, Russell dined at Castle Hill, the seat of Lord Fortescue. He was taking his leave with the children hanging on to the skirts of his coat when one of them asked him about his first day's staghunting. Russell told them and, catching sight of a head on the wall, he said "And there he is."

Although Russell's schooldays were harsh, even brutal, he had a great affection for his old school. He punctiliously attended the old boys' days and often preached in the school chapel.

At Oxford Russell's college was Exeter which was noted for classics. The new undergraduate found that few of his fellows were addicted to learning. The sons of country squires and gentlemen, most of them spent their time shooting, hunting and fishing. The head of the college, Dr. Cole, was an easy-going man and his tutors rarely interfered with the pleasures of the undergraduates, so long as chapel and lectures were attended with a modicum of regularity.

After the harsh regimen of his schooldays, this new freedom delighted Russell and he hunted with the Beaufort, the Bicester and the Old Berkshire as often as his limited means would allow. It was fortunate that his funds were low as, had he possessed the means, he would have hunted far more often and would almost certainly have failed his finals. His excuse, when asked to join a friend for a day's hunting was, "Impossible. I'm suffering from a tightness of the chest and my doctor won't let me hunt at any price."

It was at this time that Russell first saw the art of hunting a pack of foxhounds. Both Goodall of the Bicester and Philip Payne of the Beaufort were in the top class of professional huntsman. Russell watched their methods and, naturally gifted as he was, stored up all this knowledge for future use.

Russell never forgot his first day's attendance at a meet of the Beaufort. The horses went on overnight and the next day Russell and a friend rode to the meet. There was a bitter north wind blowing and the countryside was in the grip of frost. They had been at the meet for a little time when Will Long, the whipper-in, rode up. "His Grace's compliments and he begs to say that the frost is too hard to take the hounds out of kennel." he said. Russell was terribly disappointed and without thinking, he said "Then when you get back I hope you find them dead on their benches." Years later, when Long was the Beaufort huntsman, he reminded Russell of the occasion. Russell replied that two minutes later he could have cut his tongue out.

On the following day Russell went out with what is now the Bicester. They were running hard when the Duke of Beaufort's hounds appeared and the two packs joined up and had a terrific run across the best part of the Bicester Vale. "Never before," wrote Russell, "had I witnessed so glorious a run and you may well imagine the pride I felt on finding myself in such good company. Caligula never honoured his horse as I then honoured Old Charlie. I could have hugged him on the spot. As for Will Long, I looked upon him as something more than mortal, a demi-god in disguise."

Russell also took up boxing and, while not being of a pugnacious nature, he held that it was every man's duty to stand up for himself if necessary. He was not interested in racing, shooting or fishing; hunting was the great love, but next to that, being a Westcountryman, he loved wrestling. Russell used to tell of how, on a certain Sunday, while at church in Cornwall he saw a man standing outside the churchyard gate; stuck into the band of his hat were six silver spoons and he was shouting, "Plaize to tak' notiss. Thaise zix zilver spunes to be wrastled vor next Thursday at Poughill and all gen'lemen wrastling 'ull receive fair play." The man then entered the church, went up into the "singing gallery" and hung his hat on a peg where it was visible to the parson and the congregation. In later years Russell would attend the wrestling matches and so excited did he get that he would throw silver into the ring until his pockets were empty; then he would turn to his friends and beg them to lend him money to encourage the wrestlers. It is said that few of them were ever repaid.

It was perhaps lucky for Russell that the examination standards in the Oxford of his day were not nearly so high as they are today. It was imperative that he got his degree as he intended to take Holy Orders. He used to say that it was no wonder that Oxford was regarded as a seat of learning as so many men left such a lot of learning there when they went down. After putting in the requisite number of terms, the finals approached and it was the learning that he had acquired at Blundell's, rather than the studying he had done at the University that enabled him to satisfy the examiners. When he went in to the viva, he said that he felt very like Atlas, with a world of weight upon his shoulders. It was with relief that he learned that he had passed and that night he and the other successful examinees celebrated with a supper and that was the end of his Oxford career.

III

## ORDAINED

Russell was ordained a deacon in 1819 and priested the following year. He had been offered the curacy of George Nympton, near South Molton, and the double coach journey to London to be made a deacon and afterwards ordained a priest was a severe burden on an income of £60 a year, but Bishop Pelham who ordained him was not a man to consider the convenience of his clergy.

Writing of this time in Russell's life, E. W. L. Davies in *A Memoir of the Rev. John Russell* says:

"That Russell entered on the work of the ministry with a due sense of the sacred office and his own responsibility, will no doubt be charitably questioned by many who have only heard of his fame in the hunting field. But, if an ever-ready readiness to visit the sick and the world-weary; to administer consolation to all who needed it; to preach God's work with the fervour, if not the eloquence of a Bourdaloue; to plead in many a neighbouring pulpit, whenever invited to do so, the cause of charitable institutions, the funds of which never failed to derive substantial aid from his advocacy during a period of fifty years — if such things be of good report, and carry any weight, no human being can say of him — though he would be the first to say it of himself — that his mission as a Christian minister had been altogether that of an unprofitable servant."

Russell quickly found that his curacy at George Nympton engaged very little of his time. He was no scholar and loathed reading, so he gladly accepted when his rector, who was the incumbent of South Molton, asked him to take on the weekly duty of that parish. He settled at South Molton and looked after both parishes, but with no addition to his stipend of £60 a year.

Even with his additional duties, Russell found that time hung on his hands. With his love of the open air and of field sports his thoughts turned to hounds and he got together a scratch pack of five or six couple and kennelled them with various friends in the parish. He intended to hunt otter with them, but the trouble was that none of his hounds had hunted otter before and Russell himself was a tyro at the game. Not an otter could he find though he and his hound spent long days tramping the riversides of Exmoor. "I must have walked three thousand miles," he said, "without finding an otter, though I must have drawn over scores."

But these long and fruitless tramps with his little pack were not wasted. They gave him a knowledge of the country which was possessed by few other men. In years to come, on dark and starless nights, with many a long mile to ride to his kennels, he would go without hesitation over the pathless moor, over flooded streams and deep combes, to arrive safely back at his home.

Things changed for the better when Russell met a farmer who had a hound called Racer. This hound had been drafted from a pack which hunted fox, otter or hare, as he was too fast. Russell bought him for one guinea and the luck changed. It turned out that Racer had hunted an otter only once before, but he knew what it was all about and he quickly taught the little pack, so that Russell killed thirty-five otters off the reel.

For six years Russell hunted his pack of otterhounds, but the otter hunting season was confined to the summer, so in the winter he hunted with the hounds kept by the Rev. John

Froude of Knowstone. Froude was notorious for his complete disregard of all episcopal and human authority and was quite unfitted to be in Orders, but he showed good sport with his hounds and it is most probably because of this that Russell became friendly with him.

In a letter to E. W. L. Davies, Russell said, "Froude's hounds were something out of the common; bred from the old staghounds — light in their colour and sharp as needles — plenty of tongue, but would drive like furies. I have never seen a better or more killing pack in all my long life."

It is a blot upon Russell's character that he took up with such a man as Froude. The rector was a man of some intellect and wit, but his moorland parish was remote and he took up with the rougher characters and preferred their company to that of gentlefolk. His temper was awful and anyone who crossed his path soon suffered for it. He boasted that he had committed every crime in the ecclesiastical calendar. There is a wry humour in the fact that on the few occasions the Bishop tried to call him to account, it was Froude who had the better of it.

The first time the Bishop tried to nail him was when the local newspapers had been publishing articles headed *Knowstone Again* and accusing Froude of various misdemeanours. The Bishop thought Froude had been unfairly victimised and summoned him to the palace. Froude took no notice, nor did he attend the Bishop's visitations, so the Bishop went to Knowstone.

It was a bitterly cold morning when the Bishop arrived at Knowstone vicarage. On enquiring for Mr. Froude he was shown in to a room where Froude was sitting before a roaring, fire, his head muffled in flannel and his voice as hoarse as a raven.

"I've come to see you, Mr. Froude," began the Bishop, "to see if —"

"Oh, yes, my lord," interrupted Froude, "'tis cold work travelling over our moors; do 'ee take a glass of hot brandy and water, 'twill keep off the shivers."

In spite of the Bishop's protestations, Froude rang the bell and ordered a glass of hot brandy and water for his lordship. The Bishop declined the drink and endeavoured to explain the object of his visit, but Froude, apparently could not hear him. "If only I'd taken hot brandy and water when I caught my chill," he said, "I shouldn't be as I am now. Deaf as a haddock." The Bishop saw that it was no use and left. Ten minutes later Froude came out, mounted his horse, and went hunting.

Russell used to say that if the Bishop had gone to Knowstone a dozen times, the result would have been the same. To a young man like Russell, Froude's company must have been very attractive, as he was witty and hospitable. Also he was no mean exponent of the art of hunting a pack of hounds. But he had a very dark side to his character and it is no credit to Russell that he was friendly with him.

The six years during which Russell kept otterhounds at South Molton may be regarded as his apprenticeship for his later position as a Master of Foxhounds. It was at this time that he got to know Mr. George Templer of Stover who was the Master of a pack of dwarf foxhounds. Mr. Templer's system of hunting was extraordinary as he kept about twenty foxes, each one in a separate coop to which it was attached by a chain. When a fox was turned out it was always done in view of the hounds and fair law was allowed. The thing then was to save the fox alive and such was the hard riding of the followers and the obedience of the hounds that nine times out of ten the fox was picked up unharmed. How this was done without somebody being badly bitten is a mystery. One fox, called "The Bold Dragoon" had been turned out thirty-six times. Russell learned a lot from Templer's control of his hounds which was done without the aid of whipcord. A friend of his wrote: "His mode of tuition was so perfect that each hound comprehended every inflection of his voice; every note of his horn was intelligible to them and conveyed a full meaning; and to the wave of the hand an instant obedience was given that required neither rate nor sterner discipline to urge."

About the middle of the 1820s Russell fell in love. The lady was Miss Penelope Incledon Bury, the daughter of Admiral and Mrs. Bury of Dennington, near Barnstaple. The courtship was not without its mishaps. After hunting with the Rev. Harry Farr Yeatman's hounds at Stock, near Sherborne, Russell set out after dinner to visit Miss Bury, who was staying with her people at Bath, some fifty miles away. At Warminster he found it necessary to leave his own horse behind him and hire one which would carry him like an infant in a cradle. The only light was from a dim horn lantern when Russell mounted his new steed. He arrived at Bath long after midnight and took a room at the White Lion Inn. As the ostler took his horse, Russell told him, "Feed him well and bring him in the morning to No. 9 Milsom Street at eleven o'clock."

Miss Bury and one or two fashionable young men were awaiting Russell when he arrived on foot. When the ostler made his appearance leading Russell's horse there was a burst of laughter, for the animal had no mane or tail and scarcely an ounce of flesh on his bones. On his back was an old-fashioned post-boy's saddle, secured to his rat tail by a huge crupper. Russell, however, could take a laugh against himself and rode out with his lady and her attendants on what he loved to record was one of the happiest, if not the happiest, day of his long life.

He won his lady, for on May 30th, 1826, he and Miss Bury were married. It was not long afterwards that he removed from South Molton and George Nympton to Iddesleigh, near Hatherleigh, as curate under his father. This must have been an arrangement of family convenience as Iddesleigh was, as it is now, a small parish with no need for a curate. The parish is, today, much as it was in Russell's time, the cob cottages cower on the hillside round the fifteenth century church. The only difference is that the roads are better kept.

It says much for Penelope Russell's love for her husband and for her good nature that she was happy during the years they spent at Iddesleigh, although she and her husband shared the Rectory with their in-laws. Her happiness was, however, marred when she lost her first-born son as an infant, but her second son, Bury, was born a short time after.

With little or nothing to do in such a small and isolated parish Russell's thoughts inevitably turned to hunting and it was not long before he had got together a small pack of eleven or twelve couple of hounds from various sources, but mainly from the remainder of the famous Stover pack which had been disbanded after George Templer's death. The kennels of both the Rev. Peter Glubb's hounds at Torrington and the Hon. Newton Fellowes's at Eggesford were some ten miles equidistant from Iddesleigh, so that Russell had not much country to hunt. However, both these Masters of Hounds readily granted him permission to draw coverts on the fringes of their countries.

There was a bigger hurdle in front as Russell speedily found. The villagers completely ignored the sport of foxhunting and would kill a fox whenever and wherever they could. Such was the scarcity of foxes that, for the first season or two, Russell was forced to hunt hares as well.

One day, when he was drawing for a fox, Russell heard a church bell ringing. He knew that it was the signal that a fox had been tracked to its earth and the bell called the villagers to come with pick and shovel to destroy it. Russell was soon on the spot with his ten couple of hounds and found about a hundred people there, including two gentlemen. He remonstrated with them and told them that if they would leave the foxes alone, he would show them sport with his little pack. The two gentlemen then left and a few shillings judiciously distributed among the crowd caused them to disperse.

Russell was not finished with the fox-killers. The break-through came when he heard that a fox had been traced into a brake at Beaford. He let out his hounds and hurried to the place. He found only one man there whom he asked where the fox was. The man refused, but half-a-crown soon loosened his tongue and he pointed out the place where the fox was lying. Russell put it up and ran it for about half-an-hour before losing it near where it had been found.

As he was going home he met a crowd of men, women and children who were going to see the fox killed. Many of them had loaded guns and when they found that Russell had disturbed the fox their language was anything but choice. One of the principal farmers of the parish said to Russell "Who are you, sir, to spoil our sport?"

Russell replied, "You would have spoiled mine if you could . . . get a horse, come out with me, and I'll show you some fine sport if only you'll give up shooting foxes."

The farmer answered that he would shoot foxes whenever he could. At this point a hound began to howl and Russell asked who had kicked it. It turned out that it had been a little boy.

"'Tis lucky for him that he is a little boy," cried Russell, "because if a man had kicked the hound I would have horsewhipped him on the spot."

"You'd find that a difficult job" was the curt rejoinder.

Russell jumped off his horse, threw down his whip, and said "Who's the man to prevent me?" Not a word was spoken as Russell stood there glaring defiantly at the would-be vulpicides. Gradually the crowd began to melt away and, from that day forward, Russell said that he secured for himself and his successors goodwill, co-operation and friendship.

Russell's fearlessness, his charm of manner and his prowess in the hunting field gave him a great amount of influence with the farmers and villagers. A man who did some earth-stopping for him took to sheep-stealing and was caught, tried and hanged. Shortly afterwards Russell happened to meet a farmer who had been on the jury. "Surely, there was something that might be said for the poor fellow," he remarked. "You know what a quiet fellow he was; always ready to do a neighbour a good turn. T'was a pity you should have given your voice against him."

"Bless us, Mr. Russell" said the farmer. "Yeu don't zay zo. If us had only known that was your honour's thoughts, us'd have put it raight. Me Lard Judge zaid he did ought to be hanged, so us hanged un. But, if us'd only knawed your honour cared about un, us'd have put it raight in quick time."

Russell showed such excellent sport that it was not long before many of the landowners were inviting him to hunt over their land. John Morth Woolcombe, who owned a large estate called Ashbury, was enthusiastic and came out with the hounds and Russell's small country began to grow bigger and bigger. An example of his success as a huntsman is that in 1828 he found thirty-two foxes and killed twenty-eight of them. He also killed seventy-three brace of hares which were hunted when no foxes could be found.

But success brought its attendant worries. Russell received no subscription, nor, indeed, did he ask for one, so the expense of hunting the country ate very largely into his little income. Because of this he agreed to merge his pack with that of Mr. C. A. Harris of Hayne. Harris helped financially, but Russell retained the ownership of the pack and hunted them.

At the first meet of the joint pack, the field were astonished to see seventy couple of hounds round Russell's horse. These were soon reduced to thirty-five couple.

Harris was a dyed-in-the-wool hunting man and he decided to create what was known as St. Hubert's Hall. This was in a disused quarry. The centre of the quarry was paved with granite and twenty-two stalls were hollowed out. When they were used each stall had a wooden canopy above it on which was carved a fox's head, with a silver horn if the occupant was a Master of Hounds. The quarry is still there, though the stalls have long since vanished. At the opening of St. Hubert's Hall the knights of St. Hubert were installed. One of the Hayne servants had been told to bring his bugle and entertain the guests with a little music. His repertoire was limited, but the guests were amused. During the day the bugler slipped off to have a pint or two or three and during the afternoon his bugling became very uncertain.

In a report of a meet at Tetcott House in 1829 the *Sporting Magazine* said, "The meet comprised about a hundred horsemen . . . The Master of Hounds, his pack and whipper-in then appeared. The turnout was anything but splendid, the Master on a stuggy galloway, the whipper-in, who had borrowed his helmet from the Castle of Otranto for the occasion, and was, of course, nearly buried therein, was mounted on a small black pony; the pack a lot of sharp, dwarf foxhounds." The writer added that he had never seen so quick, so excellent a sportsman as Mr. Russell or a better pack than his little hounds. He also said that he thought Russell would lead the best steeplechasers anywhere.

Like all good huntsmen Russell was a good field naturalist

Honey, now dead, was by a Hertfordshire Hunt terrier out of an Oakley Hunt bitch. She was bred and owned by Mrs. Delphine Ratcliff, the daughter of Mr. Jack Ivester Lloyd, Master of the Bagley Rat Hounds. Honey was fifteen years old when the photograph was taken and still as game as they come.

(*Above*) Trilby, a broken-coated terrier bitch. This kind of all-weather coat is the best as it does not let the rain through. Trilby is owned by Mr. Peter H. Stone of Leadgate, County Durham. (*Below*) This good-looking dog is Turban, another of Mr. Stone's terriers.

and very observant. On one occasion he had drawn one of the best coverts blank when he noticed a thistle in the field. He said to a man standing by, "Want to earn a shilling? Smell the top of that thistle, then smell it all the way down." The man did so and sniffed heartily at the stem of the thistle. He was nearly at the bottom, when he gave a snort of disgust. A fox had cocked his leg there. "There's a fox here somewhere," said Russell, put his hound back into covert, found the fox, and killed him after a good hunt of one hour, forty minutes.

His control of his hounds was little short of marvellous. A farmer said of him, "It fairly maketh a man's heart jump in his waistcoat to hear Parson Rissell find his fox; twixt he and the hounds 'tis like a band of music striking up for the dance." When he doubled his horn for the "gone away" his hounds would come racing out of covert at once so that he had little need of a whipper-in.

Russell's friendly manners and his good temper quickly led to his being invited to draw coverts far from his home and it was not long before his country extended from Torrington to Bodmin in Cornwall, a distance of some seventy miles. The Cornish gentlemen welcomed Russell and his hounds to their properties and gave him a fortnight's hunting each year. He would take his little pack and stay in the country for a week as the guest of some prominent landowner. Sometimes the hunt week was shared with another pack, sometimes it was Russell alone who hunted the country.

In the evenings there would be revelry as the day was lived over again, but Russell was no wine-bibber. He used to say, "Hunting, I tell you is worth any sacrifice; and if you sit up and get a headache, you can't thoroughly enjoy it. So, by your leave, good-night, gentlemen."

In a day when the only way of travelling a long distance was on a horse or in a carriage, Russell's endurance on horseback became a by-word throughout the West Country. More than once he left Iddlesleigh before first light, rode to the Bodmin Moors, and then rode home at night. It is, of course, obvious that in those days both men and horses had to be fit and hard, but Russell's apparent insensibility to fatigue — and the endurance of his horses — were the talk of the district.

The stoutness of constitution endured right into old age. In his eighty-second year, in accordance with his usual habit, he rode to the opening meet of the Staghounds at Cloutsham and rode home at night, a distance of twenty-five miles each way. When he was seventy-nine he rode part of the way to Ivybridge — the rest of the journey was done by rail — arrived in time for the meet and hunted all day. Every day of that week at Ivybridge Russell hunted and on the Saturday he left at two o'clock and started for home. He changed horses mid-way and got home to Swymbridge that night at eleven o'clock. Before he sat down to eat he wrote a letter to his hostess saying that he had eaten nothing since the morning and that he felt neither hungry, thirsty nor tired after his journey of seventy miles. The next day he took three full services in his parish.

Mr. Fenwick-Bissett, the Master of the Staghounds owned a house at Bagborough on the Quantocks and twice a year the hunt would migrate there to hunt the Quantocks for a week. Russell was eighty years of age when he received a letter from Fenwick-Bissett inviting him to come up on the Friday, dine, and stay the night, and hunt on the Saturday. On the Friday morning Russell saddled his pony at Swymbridge and rode the forty or so miles to Bagborough. The next day he hunted and at four o'clock they killed at East Quantockshead. The Rector's wife said to him, "John, you'll come in to tea, won't you." He answered, "Thank you, Maggie, but there is no time. I have early duty to take in the morning." He turned his pony's head and rode back to Swymbridge. It was eleven o'clock when he got there and the household had gone to bed as they did not expect him. He managed to get in through the drawing-room window and the next morning the servants caught it for not locking up properly.

In Russell's third season at Iddesleigh, trouble loomed. His country had become too big for him to hunt with his slender means. There was also a certain amount of jealousy at his success — it was suggested that part of the country should be hunted by another pack of hounds and John Morth Woolcombe, who had shown such friendship, turned against Russell and killed the foxes on his estate.

Then the trustees of the Molesworth estate followed Woolcombe's lead and suggested the need for another pack of hounds. Their action is understandable when it is realised that despite Russell's activities and his success, foxes had increased and were doing damage for which Russell's purse was not large enough to pay.

Although Russell resisted the move with all his might, a Mr. Tom Phillips started another pack of hounds and took over a lot of Russell's country. The golden days were over and there was a certain amount of unpleasantness about the whole affair. But it did not last long because, in 1832, Russell was offered, and accepted, the perpetual curacy of Swymbridge and Landkey, near Barnstaple.

IV

## TO SWYMBRIDGE

Penelope Russell was delighted with the move to Swymbridge. She had been born and bred at nearby Dennington House and her widowed mother still lived there. The young couple went to live at Tordown, which stands high up above the village. Russell always referred to the house as his Alpine residence. The house was, and is, approached by a narrow and precipitous lane which, in Russell's day, was impossible for a carriage when snow or ice was on the road. The house is long and low with stables on the other side of the road.

Swymbridge cannot be called an attractive village. It is long and narrow and the only attractive thing about it is the church, the inside of which was improved when Russell began the restoration in 1889. On the font can still be seen remains of the medieval gilding and colouring and just inside the door are two photographs of John Russell.

Opposite the church stands an inn which was called the New Inn, but in recent years its name has been changed to "The Jack Russell". It has a reproduction of the portrait of Trump as its sign. Trump was the first terrier Russell ever owned, of whom more later.

In later years Russell wrote, "When I was first inducted to this incumbency, there was only one service here every Sunday morning and evening alternately with Landkey, whereas, now, I am thankful to say, we have four services every Sunday in Swymbridge alone."

When Russell was inducted the living was a poor one —
only £180 a year, so it is not surprising that Mrs. Russell
often had to come to the rescue. She loved hunting as much
as her husband did and her help was always gladly given.

The Russells were given a great welcome to Swymbridge;
Penelope because she was regarded as a native of the village,
and Russell because he was so well-known in the hunting
field. In addition to this, Russell's kindly nature and
cheerful disposition made him very popular with the farmers
over whose land he hunted. Unlike many Masters of Hounds
of the day he was never heard to swear at his field no matter
how provoked he might be. Davies says, "No man has been
more venerated — nay, loved — by the poor among whom
he ministered than Mr. Russell. And with good reason too;
for in season or out of season, no one of them in distress ever
appealed to him in vain."

This innate kindliness of Russell's is shown by his treatment of gipsies. In a day when they were treated as trespassers
and plunderers he befriended them whenever he thought
they were being unfairly used. In return the gipsies were
always careful not to give him any cause for complaint.

At one time there was an outbreak of burglaries and it
afterwards became known that the gipsies had kept watch
over Russell's house at night to make sure that it was not
broken into. Long before this, Russell had secured the
goodwill of the gipsies when a blacksmith told him that a
gipsy man wished to buy the blacksmith's mare, but he had
no money with him and wanted the smith to trust him.
Russell looked at the gipsy and noted that he had an honest
face and said, "If I pass my word for the money, will you pay
it?" The man said that he would.

"Then," said Russell to the blacksmith, "you may look to
me for the money; if he don't pay you, I will."

The gipsy did pay for the mare and ever after Russell was

regarded as a benefactor. On his deathbed the king of the gipsies left Russell a charm, a silver Spanish coin, and asked that Russell might bury him in Swymbridge churchyard. The coin is now in the Athenaeum Museum at Barnstaple.

This kindliness was typical of Russell. He was no scholar, he disliked books and he was no regular visitor of his parishioners, though he or his curate were always at hand in case of need. His religion was to him a personal thing which he showed by kindness and charity to his people. It is true that he was often absent in the hunting field, but if he was away for any length of time his curate looked after the parish.

Having disbanded his old pack when he left Iddesleigh, it was not long before Russell set about getting together some more hounds. He procured six and a half couple from the Vine Hunt, but well-meaning friends advised him that it would not be seemly for the vicar to keep hounds. Accordingly, and with a heavy heart, Russell made arrangements for these new hounds to be sent to his old pack. They were taken out of kennel to be sent off when Mrs. Russell, seeing her husband's dejected face, said, "They shan't go, John, if you don't like it. I don't see why you shouldn't have your amusement as well as other people." So back went the hounds into the kennels and Russell continued as a Master of Hounds until 1871.

The Bishop of the diocese at that time was Henry Philpotts who, as mentioned earlier, had crossed swords with Russell's father. He was enthroned at a time when the Church of England was at a very low ebb indeed. Plurality was rife and many of the clergy completely neglected their parochial duties. This was a hangover from the worldly eighteenth century, when many clergy were the younger sons of landed families and were pushed willy-nilly into the family livings. They had absolutely no vocation and little or no interest in their duties. Philpotts resolved to put matters right and he did a lot to improve the state of affairs, but he was not a likeable man as he was too dogmatic and dictatorial.

The Bishop first met Russell in 1831 and noted in his diary, "A fine young man, said to be active and useful as a clergyman and a good preacher." But the Bishop did not approve of parsons hunting and did his best to stop them. Soon after his appointment he was driving through North Devon when he saw a pack of hounds in full cry followed by a number of men in black coats. He said to his chaplain, "Alas, this neighbourhood must have been visited by some fearful epidemic. I have never seen so many men in mourning." His chaplain did not dare to tell him that they were all clergymen.

As might be expected, Russell soon earned his Bishop's disapproval. He was known to be a good and popular preacher and his lordship was anxious that Russell's ministrations should not be affected by his association with the hunting field. Russell, however, could not see that he was doing anything wrong.

After a time, the Bishop received a serious accusation against Russell and summoned him to Exeter. The charge was that Russell had refused to bury a child on the day named by the parents, as it was a hunting day. Russell asked that the child's mother be brought into the room. The bishop asked her if the charge were true. "Nit a word o' it," said she. She added that her husband had asked Russell to bury the child on a Wednesday or a Thursday, whichever was most convenient to him, and that he had buried the child on a Thursday. The bishop asked if she were not inconvenienced by keeping the body a day longer. "Not a bit o' it," she answered, "us might ha' kept un to this day. T'were but an atomy bit o' a thing."

The Bishop, finding that he would get no further with this

charge, then proceeded to examine other charges brought by the same person and found that they were all without foundation. The Bishop was so disappointed at his failure to pin any dereliction of duty on Russell that he said, "The fact still remains that you keep hounds and that your curate hunts with you. Will you give up your hounds?" Russell refused to do so.

The Bishop could not oust Russell from his benefice, into which he had been formally inducted, as he had not broken any ecclesiastical law. The curate, however, was in a different position. He had been engaged by Russell, and licensed to preach by Philpotts himself. The Bishop could, therefore, revoke his licence. He turned to Sleeman, "Your licence, Sir, I revoke and I only regret that the law does not enable me to deal with the greater offender in a far more summary way."

"I am very glad to find that you can't, my lord," said Russell, "and still happier to know that I have done nothing in contravention of the law and that the law protects me. May I ask, if you revoke Mr. Sleeman's license, who is to take duty at Landkey next Sunday?"

"Mr. Sleeman may do it."

"And who the following Sunday?" asked Russell.

"Mr. Sleeman again, if by that time you have not got another curate."

"I shall take no steps to do so and shall be very cautious about whom I admit into my church," said Russell.

On hearing about this, the inhabitants of Swymbridge sent a round robin to the Bishop in Sleeman's favour and in the event he remained at Swymbridge until he married.

The probable reason for Philpotts' continued watch on Russell's hunting activities is that he looked upon him as the protagonist of the hunting clergy. The vicar was popular and well-known and Philpotts thought that if he could stop him hunting it might deter the others. It is no exaggeration to say that there were, at that time, at least twenty clergy-men in the diocese who had packs of their own. Three of them kept foxhounds, while the others hunted hares.

Like every man engaged in public life, Russell had his enemies. It was a Mr. Nott of nearby Bydown who had made the charges against Russell. He was not anti-hunting as he kept a pack of harriers. He disliked both the Russells and made as much trouble for them as he could. The matter came to a head in 1841 when Russell brought a libel action against Nott. The claim was settled out of court, but the hostility continued because of something the Russells said about the payment of the costs of the case. Both sides wrote about it to the newspapers, which did not mend matters and neither side appeared in a favourable light. In the end Nott was nearly sent to prison for swearing an illegal oath.

Another brush with the Bishop came when, once more, Philpotts appealed to Russell to give up his hounds. Much to the Bishop's astonishment, Russell agreed. "Then here's my hand on it," said the Bishop. "With all my heart," said Russell, "I'll give up the hounds, Mrs. Russell shall keep them." The proffered hand was immediately withdrawn.

It was because he employed a curate that Russell was able to do all that he did. The story had got about that a curate had to be keen on hunting before Russell would employ him, but Davies said that the curates were allowed to hunt only when parish duties permitted.

In contradiction of this there is a story of Will Chapple, the parish clerk at Swymbridge, going into a grocer's shop at Barnstaple. The grocer asked if they had yet obtained a curate for Swymbridge. "No, Zur," said Will, "tisn't everyone as'll zuit master. Here's his advertisement." He read from the *North Devon Journal*: "Wanted: a curate for Swymbridge; must be a gentleman of orthodox and moderate views."

"Orthodox! An' what do he mean by that?" asked the grocer.

"Well," said Chapple, "I don't raightly knaw, but I rackon t'is a man as can ride purty well." This story was told by the Rev. William Hocker, Vicar of Buckerell, who overheard the conversation.

Russell's hospitality and consideration for others is shown in Davies's account of his arrival at Swymbridge. He had ridden a long distance and was tired out when he reached the village in the evening. It was the first time that he had left home and he was feeling weary and despondent. He arrived at the lodgings which had been taken for him, but he had hardly unpacked when he heard a voice asking for him and Russell walked in and bade him welcome.

"Now," said Russell, "You must come and dine with us." The dinner was ample but simple; a cod's head and shoulders from Barnstaple bay, a haunch of Exmoor mutton and an apple pudding. "What has become of your horse?" asked Russell and he was told that the horse was at the village inn. "Then he mustn't stay there another minute," Russell said and ordered the horse to be brought to his own stables.

The next morning Davies was just sitting down to breakfast when, to his surprise, a cart laden with hay and corn pulled up at the door. It was from Russell. "I will not recount the similar acts of kind consideration in various ways, which I received from him and Mrs. Russell during that happy and unclouded period of my early life passed at Swymbridge." Davies wrote.

He did, however, record one passage of arms between himself and his vicar. He was acting as whipper-in when they had a long hunt and eventually came to the River Barle at Lanacre Bridge, near Exford. The river was in spate and when one hound got into it Russell called out, "That hound will be drowned. Jump in and save him." Davies saw no danger to the hound and saw no point in jumping into the ice-cold river. The hound got out safely but a little later, when Davies rated a hound for some fault, Russell, who was evidently out of temper, said sharply, "That's only a puppy, let him alone. Don't rate him or you'll ruin him." "Don't speak to me like that," Davies answered, "or I'll never turn a hound for you again." That was the end of it and vicar and curate remained on the best of terms, but often, when Russell was near Lanacre Bridge, he would laughingly point out the spot "where Davies mutinied."

In 1845 Russell and some other Masters of Hounds founded a foxhunting club with its headquarters at South Molton. The packs of Mr. Carew and Mr. Trelawney, together with Russell's own hounds, were appointed to hunt the country in the spring and the autumn and the George Inn was to become their headquarters. During these biannual meetings every stall and every bed in South Molton was bespoken by the foxhunting gentry. Under Russell's guidance these meetings flourished for many years and great sport was shown. At dinner and in the evening, they would discuss the day's sport over and over again and when the cloth was clear a curious custom was observed. The ring of a shilling, thrown into a wine glass gave notice, that, with or without the knowledge of its owner, the auction of a horse was about to take place, the owner being allowed only one bid. If he was satisfied with the price offered he bid nothing, but if he wished to keep the animal he protected himself by bidding a sum that put an end to competition.

As has been said, Russell never stayed up to a late hour, nor did he play whist which was the great game after these dinners. "I've no money to lose myself," he said, "and should be very sorry to risk injuring my neighbour by winning his."

One thing at which Russell excelled was in the telling of

Devonshire stories. He could imitate the broad Doric and he kept the table listening enthralled as he told story after story. One of these concerned John Boyce, the rector of Shirwell, who wished to have a day's staghunting at Porlock. He told the parish clerk to announce in church that there would be no service in the afternoon. Accordingly, the clerk told an amazed congregation, "This is vor to give notiss — there be no zarvice to church this arternewn, cause Maister be a'goin' over the moor a staghuntin'."

Again, the Rev. Roope-Gilbert, rector of Stockleigh-Pomeroy, told his clerk to announce that there would be only one service a day at that church for a month, as he was going to take duty at Stockleigh-English alternately with his own parish. The clerk did so in his own peculiar way, "This is vor to give notiss — there'll be no zarvice to these church but wance a wik, cause Maister's a'goin' to zarve t'other Stockleigh and these church to all etarnity."

He also used to tell of an old woman in his own parish whose only book was a dictionary. She read it she said "because it doth explain words as it do go on."

These early days at Swymbridge must have been the happiest of Russell's life. He was married to a devoted wife, he had his little pack of hounds, and he was welcomed almost wherever he went and he travelled a great deal, for he was in constant demand as a preacher for charitable causes. His physical presence, his sonorous voice and his impressive delivery brought him a constant stream of requests to appear in the pulpit. They were never refused if it was humanly possible for Russell to accept.

On one occasion, when he was staying at Haccombe, he was asked to preach. Lady Carew was at the new organ-harmonium which produced the most extraordinary noises. When the sound died away Russell ascended to the pulpit and, with a broad smile, gave out his text, "For this relief, much thanks," and preached an excellent extempore sermon.

When he was an old man of eighty he was due to preach at Barnstaple parish church. A tremendous thunder-storm had been raging all the afternoon and no one thought that the old man would come through the pouring rain, but before the service was half over Russell arrived soaked through to the skin. His sermon was an eloquent appeal for funds for the North Devon Infirmary and the collection was a record. Although he was wet through, he afterwards rode to the station and boarded a train for Exeter.

After Russell's death, his effects were sold up and the Rev. Paul Marshall, the vicar of Oare, saw some papers blowing about in the yard. He picked them up and found that they were the manuscripts of some of Russell's sermons; each one was carefully marked with the dates it was delivered, the occasions, the name of the preacher, and the churches in which it had been delivered. It was clear that he had been in the habit of lending his sermons to his curates. Mr. Marshall said that the sermons were the work of a simple, humble man who was devoted to the welfare of his people.

Russell was strictly orthodox in his views on religion. He abhorred ceremonial and ritual and felt that religion was something that should be lived every day. His creed was to help those in trouble and kindness and charity to those less fortunate than himself.

His favourite charity was the North Devon Infirmary, for which he raised large sums of money and was at one time a governor. He was also a keen Freemason and in 1835 he was invested as Provincial Grand Chaplain.

Russell was well aware that his reputation as a hunting parson could eclipse that of the parish priest and he was always eager to refute any story that would contribute to his opinion. He saw a report in the *Exeter Gazette* of one Daniel

Yelland. It said that before he died the man sent a message to Russell. "I know I'm to die and tell John Russell I'm dying game." Russell wrote to the editor, saying that what Yelland had said was, "I wish I could see dear old Mr. Russell and that he would come over and say a prayer or two by me and say a prayer for me in church. Please tell him so."

The vicar of Swymbridge had a great understanding of the simple village people. There is a story of how he visited a farmer in his parish. The man was very ill. Russell breezed into the bedroom and spoke to him in the broad Doric he always used when talking to his people. "Well, old veller," he said, "what ails thee?"

"I be a'goin' ter die and I be a'feared that owd davvil be a'goin' ter git me."

"What's talking about," said Russell. "Hasn't robbed no man, 'ave 'ee?"

"Naw Passon."

"Allus paid thee tithe, 'asn't 'ee?"

"Ais, Passon."

"Then do 'ee tell th'owd davvil ter git back ter hell. He can't touch 'ee." And so the farmer died with a quiet mind.

By early middle life Russell had made a great reputation as a sportsman and was known over the whole of the West Country. The great houses were open to him and, with a few exceptions, he was welcome everywhere. Because of "tightness of the chest" he had several times to give up his hounds, but always he was prevailed upon by his wife and friends to start up again.

His hunting establishment was modest, as he always had to exercise the keenest economy. He hunted his own hounds and was in charge of their management and breeding. Other Masters of Hounds, with deeper pockets, would let him have a draft from their kennels. He used to say, "Let me go into a strange kennel; let me have the pick of the pack, and, first and foremost, I'll take the plain-looking ones; there is sure to be good stuff in them or they would not be there."

Russell had an inborn gift for remembering hounds; two hours in a strange kennel and he could name most of the hounds next day. Working qualities came first with him and he was always careful that his hounds came from established blood-lines. A report in the *Sporting Magazine* in 1841 said: "The hounds did their work admirably and I have seldom seen a neater pack; they are certainly small for foxhounds; the greater part of them are black, white and tan, not one yellow or white hound among them. They are accompanied by a couple of neat terriers; one of them called Tipoo is one of the most perfect dogs of his calling I have ever seen." It is probable that the so-called "Tipoo" was Russell's famous "Tip".

During the hunting season hounds were always fit and hard, could last out the longest and hardest day, and come home with their sterns up. Their Master was his own vet and bled, fired or stitched up as necessary.

Russell's slender purse meant that he could never afford to have first-class horses. The animals in his stud had to be cheap, but they also had to be sound and capable of doing a season without breaking down. Russell was a big man and rode fifteen stone, so that the horses had to be up to weight. Thoroughbreds were useless to him and he preferred a cross of an Exmoor pony mare with a half-bred stallion. One horse of his which came from this cross was "Billy", of which Mr. Harris of Hayne wrote: "Russell mounted me once on Billy and little did I anticipate the great treat in store for me. The meet was at Broadbury Castle and, thinking him a pony, I at first rode him quietly; but when the hounds began to run Billy pulled at his snaffle and, letting him go, he went with a will right up to the head as if he had said to himself,

'That's my place, and I mean to keep it,' And so he did. No bank could stop him, no pace could choke him off; he could stay all day, and go a cracker through dirt up to the very last."

Russell was often forced to make do with horses of uncertain temper which could be picked up cheaply. Two of these were Cottager and Monkey. Cottager was a biter and would make a snatch at his rider's boot. He would also go for other riders. Monkey was just as unreliable, but was a good hunter when hounds were running. On the deaths of these two horses, Russell had their skins cured and he used them to cover his armchairs. On asking his visitors to sit down he would say, "Give old Cottager a turn, he'll carry you as easily as a feather bed, and he never bites now." Or, "Try Billy, if he can't go through the dirt as he once could, he's up to any weight and he won't give you a fall."

The late Mr. Oliver Robins of Brayford told the author that his father had often spoken to him of Russell's wonderful command of his horses. "When he came to a high bank, he would dismount and scramble through the hedge while the pony waited. Then he would call the pony through after him. I wonder how on earth he trained them to do that." Because of the smallness of his stud, Russell was obliged to save his horses as much as he could. Very often he would get off and run up a hillside or a steep slope, so easing the burden upon the horse. Of course, he had his fair share of falls. The *Sporting Magazine* describes one incident, "Mr. Russell handled the hounds and did his best to show us sport, but, unfortunately, he got a rattling fall over a terrible fence; two of his ribs were smashed and he was otherwise much damaged. We carried him to Tetcott where he was bled, bedded, bolstered, bandaged, physicked, gruelled and otherwise learnedly treated."

One might think that the medical treatment was even

worse than the fall, but a week later Russell was hunting again. He was also handicapped by the lack of a regular whipper-in, although his curates took a turn when they could. His son, Bury Russell, also whipped-in on occasion.

One story of his earlier days which Russell was fond of telling concerned a visit he and his hounds had made to Porlock for a week's hunting. He stayed at the Ship Inn and on his return one evening, he was accosted by the landlady, Mrs. Smith, who said, "If you plaise, Mr. Rissell, that old scamp, Squire Tamlyn, hath been down here to forbid you from hunting over his property. Now hearken to me, sir, and us'll tackle 'un as all such vermin ought to be tackled. Ask 'un to come here and dine with 'ee tomorrow and when he'th a sot down comfortable a'fore the fire, give t'other gentlemen a wink to leave the room, and I'll come in quietly behind 'un, seize both his arms and then do you wallop 'un over his face and eyes till he sings out for mercy. I'll never let 'un go, mind, till you've a'finished with 'un, and that I'll promise 'ee." At this point Russell remonstrated with her, pointing out that it would be a gross breach of hospitality and that a summons for the assault would be sure to follow.

"But," she said, "the magistrates shan't get a word out o' me to convict you sir, if he doth get a summons; and what's more I'll tell two or three such pretty stories about 'un as he won't like to hear."

"The next day," said Russell, with the view of propitiating Mr. Tamlyn, "I wrote to him a very polite note, inviting him to dine with us, but he declined the honour, much to the disgust of Mrs. Smith who consoled herself with these words: "Well, never mind, I'll give it to 'un myself the first time I set eyes on the mean old scamp."

"And," added Russell, "I have reason to believe that she absolutely kept her word; for she was a veritable termagent — a tigress in petticoats."

But, to return to the staghunting. Russell was fearless and skilled in tackling a deer at bay. On one occasion hounds had bayed a stag in a stream at Bratton Mill. An old man, fuddled with cider, went up to and attempted to caress the animal, saying, "Sober, sober now, don't 'ee be scared, my pretty dear." The stag lunged at him and drove a brow point through the man's hand, and he would certainly have been killed had not help been at hand. Russell rushed in, collared the deer by the root of his near-side horn and dragged out the tine transfixing the man's hand. The stag and Russell then rolled over and over in the bed of the stream, the animal forcing him under a footbridge and kneeling on him. Luckily for Russell, the deer left him and stood against the wall of a house, where he was taken.

In *Bailey's Magazine* of September, 1874, there was an article entitled "A Day with the Devon and Somerset Staghounds". It says: "Then comes the parson of the hunt — what westcountryman does not know, without my naming him, the best and keenest of sportsmen? Up he comes with a smile and a joke for all. As he answers the humorous greetings, I catch his cheery acknowledgements: 'Very well, thank 'ee. How's the missis? Long ride for an old fellow like me, eh? Rode all the way from home this morning — a good thirty mile and more. Going to ride all the way back, too. Hullo, that's your little girl? Your first day, my dear? . . . Follow me and you shall see the kill. Oh, I'll take care of her, never fear.' So I see the plucky little girl made utterly happy — she is to be piloted over the moor by the Rev. . . . and her joy is complete." Russell was then 79 years old.

When he was 82 Russell drove in a chaise to the opening meet of the staghounds at Cloutsham. So unusual a sight was it to see Russell in a carriage that it attracted great attention. On hunting farmer said: "Zee! There he go'th, Passen Rissell in a chaise; never zee'd 'un afore off a horse's back, never. But there, us must all come to't; yew can't have two vorenoons to one day." On the following Friday Russell attended a meet at Hawkcombe Head, 25 miles from Swymbridge, and this time he was mounted. He got home at half-past ten without any sign of exhaustion.

In 1873 Russell spent a week in Norfolk at the home of Mr. Henry Villebois and there he met the Prince of Wales, who invited him to the ball at Sandringham House. Russell danced until four in the morning and then caught the first train to London. The country parson must have made an impression on the Prince and Princess because Russell was invited to Sandringham for Christmas week. The tenants' ball was held on New Year's Eve. A little before midnight Russell was told that the Princess wished to dance the old year out with him. As the clock struck twelve, Russell said to her, "Now I can say what no man else can ever say again."

"And what may that be?" asked the Princess.

"That I've had the honour of dancing out the old year and dancing in the new with Your Royal Highness."

At dinner, on the first day of his visit, Russell's old-fashioned manners cropped up. He had been served with fish and, wishing for more, had sent his plate for a second helping. The Prince asked him if he liked fish. "Yes, sir," replied Russell, "I'm very fond of fish and I've sent up my plate a second time; and now I remember that's the very thing my wife charged me on leaving home not to do." After this the Prince saw to it that Russell always got a second helping of fish.

In 1875 Russell suffered the heaviest blow of his long life in the death of his wife Penelope. He was overwhelmed with grief. He wrote to Davies: "I am at home, again, though it no longer seems like home to me, for there is a vacant chair in every room, never again to be filled by her, the dear old soul, to whom I was united forty-nine years ago . . . if the sympathy of friendship could soothe my grief, I possess it to a very great extent; for I have received upwards of a hundred letters of comfort and condolence from friends far and near. Among them one from the Prince of Wales, most kindly and feelingly expressed."

The old man sought to assuage his grief by work. He preached for charitable institutions and so much were his services appreciated that he was made an honorary governor of the North Devon Infirmary. He wrote to Davies: "I am worked to death at this season of the year (November); going about from church to church on working days as well as Sundays, preaching and begging for the North Devon Infirmary and similar institutions and finding, when I come home, heaps of letters to answer, but no one to cheer me in my labour — alone, alone."

In 1876 Russell again paid a visit to Sandringham and extracted a promise from the Prince that he would come down to Exmoor to have a day with the Devon and Somerset Staghounds. However, at the time the Prince was supposed to come down, one of his sons had a serious illness and the visit was postponed, but in 1889 His Royal Highness came to stay with Mr. Luttrell at Dunster Castle.

Because of an outbreak of hydrophobia in the kennels the entire pack of the staghounds had been destroyed and Arthur Heal, the huntsman, had to break in an entirely new lot of hounds. There were some fears that there might be trouble with sheep, but on the day, all went well.

Dunster was decorated with flags and the whole population turned out to see the Prince arrive. Outside the little station tenants of the estate lined up to form a mounted escort. When the Prince entered the carriage the coachman, carried away with excitement, whipped up the horses and galloped off. The mounted escort had to ride for all their worth to keep up.

Although the night had been rainy, the following day was fine. Exmoor was agog. From all parts of the moor carts full of people came to the meet at Hawkcombe Head. It was estimated that there were some two thousand riders and nine thousand foot-followers. When the Prince's carriage came through Porlock, it was seen that Russell was sitting in it. Passing the Ship Inn, scene of his conversation with Mrs. Smith years before, Russell took off his hat to the new landlady and called out "Good morning, Mrs. Pulsford."

"I were so overcome, I almost forgot to curtsey," she said afterwards.

The crowd was so great that Arthur Heal could not induce a stag to go away from the Culbone Woodlands. But Mr. Nicholas Snow, the Squire of Oare, said he knew of a warrantable stag on the forest which was duly roused and the pack laid on. The Prince was piloted by Mr. Snow and John Russell, but he got into a wet place which is known as "Prince's Bog" to this day. It was a great hunt over the forest and when the stag was bayed in Badgworthy Water, the Prince was there.

Arthur Heal handed the Prince a knife and, wading into the water, the Prince stabbed the deer to the heart. Death was instantaneous and he explained to Heal that that was the Scottish way of doing it. The Prince and a few riders then went to Oare Manor to take tea with Nicholas Snow.

That evening it is said that there was a rumour in London that the Prince had committed suicide as an evening paper had the headline, "Stag killed in Badgworthy. Prince of Wales cut his throat." Later the same evening, Dick Ridler, the butcher of Porlock was cutting up the carcase of the deer to send a haunch to Windsor Castle. "Make way," he called, "I'm cutting a haunch of venison to be sent to Her Majesty, Queen Victoria."

In addition to his parochial duties and his hunting,

Russell took a great interest in agriculture in which he took an active part. He was a founder member of the Devon Agricultural Society. These societies did an enormous amount of good. Agriculture was in a state of depression, prices had fallen, but rents remained high. There was much unemployment in the country places and wages were disgracefully low. Any man out of work had no dole, his only hope was the charity of the Parish Overseers, who allowed him and his family barely enough to keep body and soul together. As an instance of this, one old lady named Salome Friendship had to live on four shillings a week from the Overseers and one shilling from a day's washing and ironing at a local farm. The agricultural societies helped matters by holding shows at which new ideas could be exchanged and which helped to improve the quality of farm stock.

Russell was also an active member of the North Molton and Twitchen Agricultural Society, the activities of which included a ploughing match which attracted people from miles around. In the evening, they all adjourned to the local inn for dinner at which Russell was always a speaker. Another speaker was Mr. Quartly of Great Champson, Molland, who was the originator of the Red Devon breed of cattle, the "Red Rubies" as they are known.

Another interest of Russell's was the North Devon Wool Fair. The first one was held in 1863 and it attracted such notices that the following year, manufacturers came from the north to buy. He was also president of the North Tawton, Swymbridge and Landkey Agricultural Society and took the chair at their dinners.

Russell was a shareholder in the East Combe Silver Mine near Swymbridge. A water wheel was erected and Mrs. Russell broke a bottle of wine over it as she named it "Mary Ann". But the mine was not successful and Russell must have lost money which he could ill afford. Another project in which he also probably lost money was the Devon and Somerset Railway Company, formed to help communication between Barnstaple and Exeter. Despite the celebrations at the opening of the line, its finances were always in a perilous state and shareholders lost a lot of their capital.

It is not generally known that Russell may fairly be called the founder of the present day Exmoor Foxhounds. Mr. Nicholas Snow had acquired a little pack of harriers from a Mr. Phelps of Porlock who had hunted hares and polecats with them. The pack was kenneled near Porlock church and neighbours complained about the noise that the hounds made, so Phelps was forced to give them up. Squire Snow took them on and he also hunted hares until one day in 1869 they were drawing Brendon Common without success when Russell called out, "Nicholas, have done with this. Go and draw for a fox." Mr. Snow did so, they found a fox, had a splendid run with a kill at the end and thenceforward they hunted fox and fox only. They were known by the lovely name of The Stars of the West.

It was not until 1871 that Parson John gave up his hounds for, what he thought was, the last time. He parted with them to Mr. Henry Villebois through whom Russell had come to know the Prince of Wales.

The last years of Russell's life could not have been happy ones. He continued to hunt, he travelled and visited the county families, but at home he was alone. His son, Bury, was constantly in financial difficulties and eventually became bankrupt though he later became a bank manager at Barnstaple. It is reasonable to suppose that his father helped him as much as he could out of his slender resources.

In addition to these worries, Russell had financial trouble so that, when Lord Poltimore offered him the living of Black Torrington in 1879, he was forced to accept, though it meant leaving Swymbridge and his beloved Exmoor.

V

# BLACK TORRINGTON

In 1879 Russell was eighty-four. He had spent the best part of fifty years at Swymbridge he could hardly bear to leave. He wrote to Davies, "Tell me, my dear old friend, what *shall* I do about Black Torrington? I cannot live on £220 a year, which is all I shall have after I have paid a certain annuity for another three or four years. Black Torrington is a clear £500 a year and there is a good house; but then it is neither Tordown nor Exmoor; and by the time I am settled in there I shall, perhaps, be called upon to leave it again for Swymbridge churchyard. What shall I do? How can I leave my own people, with whom I have lived in peace and happiness for half a century? It will be a bitter pill to swallow, if it must be taken; but it will be my poverty and not my will that will consent to it."

His poverty forced his hand and he accepted the living of Black Torrington. He wrote again to Davies, "The day of my departure from my happy home draweth nigh and I am fretting myself to death about leaving it. Old John Squire of Ascot told me on Friday that if I went from Swymbridge it wouldn't be long before I was brought back again. Cheering — very, eh? But possibly too true to be pleasant." The people of Swymbridge were just as sad about the old man's departure. He had been with them so long that they had thought he would end his days among them; but it was not to be.

To show their appreciation of his work and of their

affection for him a testimonial was got up, subscribed to by both his parishioners and his friends. The Prince of Wales contributed and the final sum amounted to nearly £800. Russell was given a silver soup tureen and a cheque for the rest of the money. The presentation was made by Lord Fortescue. Russell nearly broke down when he replied, "I must plead for your kind indulgence to me today. My heart is full and you will, I hope, pardon its overflowing. I know well that my poor tongue will utterly fail in any way adequately to express the depth of my gratitude for the honour now bestowed upon me."

Russell gave his last sermon at Swymbridge, when he travelled from Torrington to preach when the church was re-opened in 1879 after restoration. As he saw it then it still is today. During Parson John's long ministry a chapel of rest had been erected at Traveller's Rest and a new school built and endowed, both of them with money raised by Russell.

The Bishop of Exeter, the great Dr. Temple, who afterwards became Archbishop of Canterbury, came to the re-opening of Swymbridge church. He said, "I am exceedingly pleased to see such a gathering as we have here, showing such hearty good will, such unanimity of feeling in the parish, so very much that has bound all your hearts together. And I must also say that it indicates that your late vicar has somehow or other found the way to your hearts in the discharge of his duties. I have always had a very warm regard for him; have always been ready to recognise in him a very hearty, true and conscientious man, a very warm friend, and a very careful doer of all the duties he has undertaken. And now that he has gone away, it is a great satisfaction that those who knew him when he was here, should be so ready to gather round him on the occasion of the completion of a work which he has taken up with great heartiness and which he has done so much to bring to an admirable completion." Temple had a great liking for Russell and regarded him as a good parish priest. Once, when someone said that Russell hunted too much, Temple replied, "If all the parishes in my diocese were worked as well as Mr. Russell's, I should not have all the worry that I now have."

Russell's fame had preceded him to Black Torrington and he was given a very hearty welcome to his new parish. The church bells were rung and he stayed with a local worthy until his house was ready. But he was not happy. Black Torrington was way off the beaten track and the old man missed his life-long friends of Exmoor. He had completed the decoration of his new house and built new stables when fire broke out and the stables were completely destroyed. He wrote, "I had only just completed them, and at my own expense, when in less than an hour and a half they became a heap of ruins. There were two horses besides two terriers. Alas, they are all dead."

Mary Cocking, his faithful housekeeper, did her best for the old man, but he was lonely and pined for Exmoor. Mary had been with Russell since, as a child, he had taken her out of a charity school, and she remained in his service until his death. He did not forget her in his will and she inherited a large share of the little money that remained.

In his loneliness and unhappiness Russell turned again to hounds and got together a pack of eight couple of harriers. He had no whipper-in, but in a very short time he had his hounds under complete control. Hares were scarce and there were many blank days, but Russell carried on under conditions which would have disheartened many another man. He lost three hounds which were poisoned by strychnine and he wrote to a friend, "I am living among back-biters, poisoners and fox trappers . . . "

His health was failing, but he still rode great distances

which would have daunted many other men. When he was eighty-three, he had a bad fall when out with the Staghounds. Both he and his horse rolled down to the bottom of a combe. It was nearly half an hour before he could speak, but he then climbed back on to his horse and rode six miles home.

Earlier in life, he had written to Davies, telling him of what he had just done. "I left Tordown on one eventful morning, rode to Iddesleigh (twenty miles) whither I had sent the hounds the evening before, found a fox and killed him during one of the most awful storms of rain, thunder and lightning I ever saw . . . I then rode to Ash, Mr. Mallett's place, dined there and danced afterwards till one o'clock, went to bed and rose again at three; pulled on my top boots and rode down to Bodmin, just fifty miles and met Tom Hext's hounds . . . Found a good fox and killed him; dined with my old friend Pomeroy Gilbert, and again did not get to bed, much against my rule, till the little hours. Rested the next day, if walking several miles to a country fair can be called resting; then off next morning at three; rode back to Iddesleigh, took out the hounds, found a fox in Dowland and killed him close to the Schoolmaster Inn in Chawleigh parish, twelve miles as the crow flies. I then turned my horse's head for Tordown, and was sitting down to dinner at my own table, and all the hounds home at six o'clock, the distance being fully twenty miles from the said Schoolmaster Inn to this house." Is it any wonder that Russell was looked upon with awe by all the sportsmen of the Westcountry?

In *Bailey's Magazine* for November 1885, an unsigned article gives a picture of Russell's last days at Black Torrington: "Here is the village shop at last, and down the hill we go, past the blacksmith's and turn sharply to the left through a gate under some waving trees into the presence of the Rector. He stands on the doorstep with a courteous welcome to the descending guests . . . There sits our venerable host behind his flagon, carving with a liberal hand, and continually calling his housekeeper, Mary, to his aid. From the flower garden, then scarcely a suggestion of what had been, you could hear the yelping of hounds across the roads in their spacious yard adjoining the church-yard . . ."

After morning service the next day, the visitors were taken to see the hounds. "I never dare raise my voice near the yard on Sundays," said Russell. Later on he told his visitors, "Do you know what an escape you have had? The yard door was left open and Mary spied the hounds in the act of starting on my track to church."

The article says that in church the prayers could scarcely have been read with more intelligence and beautiful distinctness and the clearly-arranged discourses of the old school type had that unmistakeable ring of reliablity inseparable from Russell's nature.

Russell kept several dogs in the house. One of them called "Rags" had lost an eye in a fight with a cat. The other three terriers were "Sly", "Fuss" and "Tinker". There was also a collie which had belonged to Mrs. Russell and was therefore much loved. The rooms of the rectory were full of brushes, masks and antlers, crowded together in typically Victorian fashion. There were also many sporting pictures, Russell's favourite being one of his wife on her mare.

The author of the article says that as Russell got old and weak he would lie in bed with his Bible and Greek Testament beside him, expressing the faith and confidence of a little child. One Christmas he gave a dinner for the tradesmen of his parish. The proposer of his health said how good it was to see so many religious denominations round the table. Russell replied that he expected all the members

of his parish to attend some place of worship and that
anyone who did not worship God was detestable and he
refused to have any dealings with him.

He loved children and soon after he arrived in Black
Torrington he gave a tea for two hundred of them — church
and chapel — and gave each child a little present. The old
man never missed an Old Boys Day at Blundell's, his old
school. He always spoke at these meetings and very often
preached a sermon. At one such gathering he recalled how
he had visited Dr. Richards, his old headmaster who had hit
so hard. Now, when Richards was a very old man, he told
Russell how as a boy he had liked to shoot rooks. Russell told
him that if the boys at Blundell's had tried that, Richards
would have knocked them down like a row of ninepins!

The wonderful stamina which had enabled Russell to
perform such prodigious feats of endurance was failing at
last and the very old man grew progressively weaker. He had
parted with his last pack of hounds to Henry Villebois,
which upset him very much, but he must have known that
the end was not far off.

He went to stay with his old friend J. C. Hawker at East
Anstey, but the moorland air did him no good. His niece,
Miss Riccard, went to the rectory to help Mary care for him.
Among the many letters he received was one from the Prince
of Wales hoping that he was recovering.

The old man wrote to Davies, "I fear we shall never meet
again. I don't gain strength as I fancy I ought; and
overwhelmed as I am by letters, it is pain and grief for me to
write at all."

On his way back from East Anstey he called at
Swymbridge and visited the church, but he had to be helped
up the path. He wrote to Hawker: "We got here at 6.30 last
evening and met half the village about 500 yards from
home, carrying flags, etc., in procession and entreating us to

allow them to remove the horses from the "fly" and draw us to the door of this house — but I declined the honour, tho' the offer was very gratifying and the reception very flattering — I was very happy with the Smyth family at Swymbridge, and was able to remain in the church and vestry during the whole of morning service on Sunday. The former is worth seeing now that it has been restored . . . "

On the advice of Dr. Linnington Ash, Russell then went to Bude in the hope that the change would improve his condition. But it was not to be and the end came on April 28th, 1883. He was in his 88th year.

# PART TWO

# THE TERRIERS

## VI

## THE BEGINNING

It was towards the end of his time at Oxford that Russell acquired his first terrier, the famous Trump. It was on a lovely May afternoon in 1819 that, Horace in hand, he walked towards Marston. Before he reached there he met a milkman and this milkman had a terrier with him. It was such an animal as Russell had seen only in his dreams of the perfect terrier. He bought her on the spot and she became the progenitress of his famous type of terrier.

An oil-painting of Trump was made and E. W. L. Davies possessed a copy of it. This painting, from which the reproduction was made for the sign at The Jack Russell pub mentioned earlier, was said by Russell to be not only an admirable likeness of the original, but also equally good as a type of the race in general. Davies never saw Trump, but here is his description of the portrait: "In the first place the colour is white with just a patch of dark tan over each eye and ear, while a similar dot, not larger than a penny piece marks the root of the tail. The coat, which is thick, close and a trifle wiry, is well calculated to protect the body from wet and cold, but has no affinity with the long, rough jacket of a Scotch terrier. The legs are straight as arrows, the feet perfect; the loins and conformation of the whole frame indicative of hardihood and endurance; while the size and height of the animal may be compared to that of a full-grown vixen fox."

Davies goes on to add that in later life Russell said that he seldom or ever saw a real fox-terrier. He was at a dog show with a hundred and fifty entries in the fox-terrier classes at the time.

Russell stated that, "They have so intermingled strange blood with the real article that, if he were not informed, it would puzzle Professor Bell himself to discover what race the so-called fox-terrier belongs to."

"And how is that managed?" asked a friend. "I can well remember Rubie's and Tom French's Dartmoor terriers and have myself owned some of that sort worth their weight in gold."

"True terriers they were" said Russell, "but differing from the present show dogs as the wild eglantine differs from a garden rose. The process is simply as follows; they begin with a smooth bitch terrier; then to obtain a finer skin, an Italian greyhound is selected as her mate. But as the ears of the produce are an eyesore to the connoisseur, a beagle is resorted to, and then little is seen of that defect in the next generation; lastly, to complete the mixture, the bulldog is called in to give the necessary courage; and the composite animals, thus elaborated, become after due selection the sires and dams of the modern fox-terrier."

The bulldog blood gave courage, but too much of it. The old pit-dogs were bred to kill and a proportion of their blood in a terrier makes the dog too hard. He goes in a hole to kill and not to bolt the fox.

Like most hunting men of his day, Russell regarded the show dogs with suspicion. His standard was gameness and not the perfection of the show-ring. However, he was a founder member of the Kennel Club, which he joined in 1873 and he judged fox-terriers at the Kennel Club show at the Crystal Palace in 1874. In 1862 he showed at the Bath and West at Exeter. The Hon. Mark Rolle took the first and third places and Russell was second. He also judged at a dog show at Bideford the following year. At this time Russell judged terriers at a great many shows, but he soon gave it up, although he remained a member of the Kennel Club until his death. He always held that a terrier had a job of work to do and was essentially a sporting dog. His dislike of the show dogs arose from the fact that they were too valuable to be given a chance to prove themselves. Terriers had become so popular that prize-winners changed hands for large sums and the owners would not risk their dogs getting scarred and so marring their perfection. This, of course, is not to say that some show dogs were not as game as their brothers which lived in foxhound kennels.

Russell neither cropped nor docked his terriers. He said of Trump that she was the first and last terrier he ever owned with cut ears and tail. He liked his dogs to have their tails on as, when one was to ground, he had something to get hold of to pull the dog out. If one pulls a dog by the hind-legs, one can permanently damage his back.

In his book *Dogs of Britain* Clifford describes a Russell terrier: "The head is broad and powerfully muscled at the cheeks; the eyes are dark and medium in size; the ears are set high, carried over to the front or side; the muzzle is powerful with even mouth. The coat is short, thick and close, usually wiry in texture, although some smooth-haired dogs appear occasionally in litters. The colour is white predominating with tan, black or lemon points about the eyes and on the set-on. Too much black or tan is disapproved of, as white is the most useful colour when the dog is working against fox or otter. Height is fourteen inches and weight sixteen pounds for dogs and fourteen pounds for bitches."

H. Compton wrote early in this century that the wire-haired terriers were not nearly so popular as the smooths until 1892: "And yet the wire-haired terrier was the Rev. John Russell's breed, and what does that not imply? For where shall you find any terrier strain, or for that matter any strain of dogs, so honoured and renowned as that of the Devonshire Parson, whose distaste for show-dogs was almost as profound as his admiration for working ones? I suppose he is the only terrier fancier who obtained a world-wide reputation for his stock without the aid of red tickets and championship certificates . . . He was as particular about the pedigrees of his own dogs as the most expert and success-ful of modern exhibitors, and only once admitted an outcross, when he imported a dash of old blood from Old Jock.

"Parson Russell's terriers were on the small side, the dogs seldom exceeding eighteen pounds and the bitches running two or three pounds less. Some of their blood is still to be found in the South West of England, but it is not so apparent in our stud books as the fame of it would have warranted."

It seems to be true that Russell never went outside the West Country for new blood with one exception. In Rawdon Lee's monograph *The Fox Terrier*, which was published in the 1890's, there is proof that at least on one occasion Russell did go outside the West for an outcross. Among the early terriers to win honours on the show bench were Old Jock, Old Tartar, Old Trap and Grove Nettle, the progenitors of most modern fox-terriers. Old Jock and Old Tartar were the ones that Russell used. Rawdon Lee quotes a letter from Russell to Mr. T. Wootton, the owner of both Jock and Tartar. "I have put one bitch to Jock and shall put another — although she is only nine months old — a rather precocious young lady you will say — tomorrow or next day; and Lord Portsmouth's huntsman will send on to him on Saturday. I have him this bitch — she is seven years old and of my purest blood, and I hope she may not miss. I never saw a sweeter animal than Jock, so perfect in shape, so much quality. He is as near perfection as we poor mortals are ever allowed to feast our eyes on. His temper is so beautiful and his pluck undeniable, for I had to choke him off a fox. You will naturally ask how I came to know about his pluck: I will tell you. Since they came here I have kept both Tartar and Jock chained up in two separate loose boxes, because they are warmer than the kennels. Yesterday morning I gave Jock a run before I went to meet the hounds and after my return from hunting I did the same office for Tartar. He went with me very kindly, as he had very frequently done before; indeed they both recognised my voice and were mad to come to me whenever they heard it; when suddenly without the least provocation, he started back and ran full tilt back to the stable, the door of which was open, and in one moment fastened upon Jock. I caught hold of him immediately, put his foot in my mouth, and bit it with all my force, choking him with my left hand at the same time; and no harm — or very little — would have happened had not Jock resented the insult and had him across the nose. This enabled Tartar, when I had freed him from Jock's foreleg, to seize his hind-leg. But I soon released him and took Jock in my arms. Tartar fastened on my servant and bit him severely. The whole thing has annoyed me dreadfully, and I am sure you will believe jealousy is the cause of the mischief."

Old Jock was bred by Jack Morgan, whipper-in to the Grove Hunt and was pupped in 1859. He was about eighteen pounds weight with a dun mark on one ear, a black patch on his stern and at its root. He stood a little high on his legs, his ribs were well sprung and his shoulders and neck nicely placed. To some he seemed a trifle loaded in the shoulders; his forelegs, feet and strength of bone were good and he had good strong jaws.

Tartar was a hardy-looking dog and he twice beat Jock at shows. He was seventeen pounds in weight and was pure white, except for a patch of pale tan over one eye. He was a trifle wide in front, but was a little straighter than Jock and with better feet. It is not known how Tartar was bred; he was shown at Birmingham in 1863 as pedigreeless.

Jock's fame was nationwide and he changed hands several times, once at the price of £100, which was big money in those days. He was bred at the Grove Hunt Kennels.

In a book, *The Dog*, published in 1872, the then editor of the *Field*, "Stonehenge" said, "The Rev. John Russell was long famous for his strain of rough terriers, so closely resembling the modern dogs exhibited by Mr. Sanderson, Mr. Carrick and Mr. Lindsay Hogg as to be inseparable by any ordinary test."

From this it is clear that Russell's terriers were similar in conformation to dogs which won on the show bench; they were recognised by the Kennel Club as they came under the generic term of "fox-terrier". It must be stressed that in Russell's day, the difference between rough and smooth terriers was not so wide as it became later on. This can be seen by studying old prints and photographs. The main difference was not in length of coat but of texture, the rough-coats being of a harder, pin-wire nature.

In the past there has been — and no doubt, there will always be — controversy about whether Russell terriers were really true bred. There is evidence on both sides. For instance, Captain G. Percival Williams, who was Master of the Fourburrow Hounds for a great many years, has said that Russell used to go down to Cornwall every year to stay with his grandfather, George Williams, at Scorrier. Captain Williams says that Russell was a terrier *dealer* and, on leaving, always asked if there were any terriers to spare. He would be told that if there were any at the kennels that they did not want, he could have them. Russell would then collect terriers on his way back to Exmoor from anyone who would let him have them.

Lord Poltimore said that his father-in-law, the late Hon. Gerald Lascelles, who was for many years Deputy Surveyor of the New Forest, was told by Russell that he had no particular breed of terrier, but that if he came across a likely dog and it was game, he would buy it and breed from it.

The late Miss Guest, who hunted her own pack of hounds for many years said that she believed that the Russell terrier was an old-fashioned working sort and that Russell bought and bred from any terrier with gameness, but she believed that he carefully kept all their pedigrees.

Mr. J. Moore-Stevens of Brompton Regis, in Somerset, whose father was a great friend of Russell's is very forthright about it. He says that Russell was nothing but an old dog-dealer. He possesses a scale model of Tip and also Russell's hunting horn.

The late Lorna, Countess Howe, wrote that Russell was a great friend of her grandfather, Mr. Bassett of Watermouth Castle in Devon. When Russell died Mr. Bassett acquired some of his terriers. She did not think that they were any sort of terrier as they were carefully bred and were of the same type. She added that Russell kept very careful pedigrees and she had seen one of his pedigree books.

Miss Begbie, a modern Jack Russell breeder, is certain that the Russell terriers were carefully bred. This was also the view of the late Arthur Heinemann, who in the early years of this century, had one of the largest kennels of working terriers in the country. Of him, more later.

The late Miss Mary Russell, John Russell's granddaughter, told the author that her grandfather's terriers were very carefully bred and that the line was kept pure. She also said that he kept meticulous pedigree books.

These directly opposed opinions can always be relied upon to produce an argument among terrier enthusiasts. Peering back through the mists of ninety years, one can form an opinion that perhaps both sides are right. Might it not be that the terriers which Russell kept and used with his hounds were very carefully bred and, that, owing to the slenderness of his purse, he also bought likely terriers and sold them at a profit? This explanation would seem to fill both sides of the bill. We will never know the truth as all his pedigree books have disappeared and there is nobody left who knew him. All the evidence we have is, of necessity, at second or third hand.

Russell placed the temperament and courage of his terriers on a par with their conformation. A working terrier must have plenty of courage, but it must be tempered with discretion. A hard dog which goes to ground and gets hold of his fox is of little use to anybody. The fox cannot bolt, it is difficult to hear the dog, and he will spend half his time in hospital. Also if another hard terrier manages to slip his lead and get to ground, the two will fight to the death.

Russell liked his dogs to find their fox underground by scent and then lie a little way away and bay him and keep on baying. Now and again the dog would dart in, nip his fox, and get back out of danger. Thus the fox was not injured and, on bolting, would give a run to the hounds. The Russell terriers were entered to fox and fox only. The parson used to say that they never tasted blood, if they did it tended to make them too hard.

Many tales were told of the sagacity and almost human reasoning power of the terriers. A favourite story of Russell's was retold by Davies; the incident happened at Lidcote Hall at Brayford in North Devon. "Do you see," said Russell, "that dark patch of hanging gorse hemmed in on the northern side by yonder knoll? Well, I've seen many a good run from that sheltered nook. On one occasion, however, I had found a fox which, in spite of a trimming scent, contrived to beat us by reaching Gray's Holt and going to ground before we could catch him. Now, those earths are as fathomless and interminable as the Catacombs of St. Calixtus. They are so called 'Gray' from the old Devonshire name signifying a badger, a number of those animals having long occupied the spot. Consequently, such a fortress once gained, is not easily to be stormed, even by Tip or the stoutest foe.

"Again we found that fox a second time; and now, while the hounds were in close pursuit and driving hard, to my infinite surprise I saw Tip going off at full speed in quite a different direction. 'He's off, Sir, to Gray's Holts. I know he is', shouted Jack Yelland, the whip, as he called my attention to the line of country the dog was taking.

"That proved to be the case. The fox had scarcely been ten minutes on foot, when the dog, either by instinct or, as I believe, by some power akin to reasoning, putting two and two together, came to the conclusion that the real object of the fox was to gain Gray's Holts, although the hounds were by no means pointing in that direction. It was exactly as if the dog had said to himself, 'No, no! You're the said fox, I know, that gave us the slip once before; but you're not going to play us that trick again.'

"Tip's deduction was accurately correct; for the fox, after a turn or two in covert, put his nose directly for Gray's Holts; hoping beyond a doubt to gain that city of refuge once more, and then to whisk his brush in the faces of his foes. But in this manoeuvre he was fairly out-generalled by the dog's tactics. Tip had taken the short cut — the chord of the arc — and as the hounds raced by at some distance off, there I saw him, dancing about on Gray's Holts, throwing his tongue frantically, and doing his utmost by noise and gesture to scare away the fox from approaching the earths.

"Perfect success crowned the manoeuvre, the fox not daring to face the lion in his path, gave the spot a wide berth, while the hounds, carrying a fine head, passed on to the heather, and after a clinking run killed him on the moor."

Tip hardly missed a day's hunting for several seasons and never appeared in the least tired, although he occasionally trotted from fifteen to twenty miles to covert. He died from asthma while to ground. Russell dug up to him and the fox in half an hour, but the old dog was dead, much to his master's grief.

One peculiarity of Tip's was that on a hunting morning nobody could catch him, once he had seen Russell with his hunting boots on. Nelson, too, did not know what fear was. He had lost an eye in a fight with a cat, but this did not deter him. Russell had run a fox to ground near Tetcott. It was a honeycomb of passages, one underneath the other and the terriers were completely unable to find the fox. At length, Nelson came out and began digging eagerly at the turf. "Here's the fox," said Russell "under Nelson's nose, or I'll forfeit my head." The dog went in the earth again and they soon heard him baying under the spot where he had been digging. The men dug in and speedily came up to the fox. Russell drew him out and let him go and treated his field to a sharp ten minutes.

Davies says that Russell looked upon his terriers as his fireside friends. He was never happier than telling and re-telling the tales of their exploits. Of course, most of them had to live in kennels, but a few of his special favourites lived in the house with him.

Idstone, a prominent sporting journalist of the 1880s, wrote: "I have seen charming terriers bred by Mr. Russell, which I know were thoroughly game and hardy and I have one which has run with hounds for three seasons. In the severest run he was always at the heels of the huntsman's horse and, if he has a fault, it is that he is a trifle too hard-bitten. But for this I think he would not have come to me. I shall state the good and bad of him without flattering of favour.

"He is white with a blue-black pair of ears, one black eye and a black nose. A sort of smutty black extends from the nose halfway to the eyes as though his nose had been smudged. He is rather leggy, but perhaps that is not a very great objection, considering that he has to run with hounds. He is rather narrow in the chest, which, as I believe, gives speed to dog or horse. At any rate, I never saw a fast animal with a wide chest.

"He has a rough or semi-brush tail and this is an eyesore to me and greatly disfigures him. (It will be remembered that Russell never docked his terriers.) His feet and legs are good, ribs round, neck long and muscular, shoulders a little too upright, loin very good, a trifle wheel-backed, which I like, and his back ribs admirable and deep.

"I should say he is about thirteen pounds weight. His countenance is a little too blunt for beauty, and it is covered in hair as close and short as a pointer's. His ears are short and thin and fall close to his head. The coat is rather long, very hard or harsh and yet perfectly smooth; his legs are very clean and the whole profile of the dog is sharp and defined when he sets up his hackles.

"I am given to understand that this dog is of the pure blood which Mr. Russell had bred for forty years or more, but I am not quite sure whether there is not some cross which would account for the rough stern and the slight coarseness in the form of his face, which I have referred to."

Although Russell's terriers ran with hounds, he would give them a lift if he thought they needed it. Old Mr. Robins said that many a time he had seen Russell returning from hunting at the end of a hard day, with a terrier perched on the horse in front of him.

From the foregoing, it can be seen that information about

the original Russell terriers is comparatively scanty, but there is quite enough for us to form a mental picture of their make and shape. The conformation of Trump is always quoted, but it must be remembered that her conformation was the ideal that Russell had in his mind. To modern eyes it would seem that some of his terriers were on the heavy side, as it is usually reckoned that a dog of sixteen pounds is quite heavy enough.

Russell's country was a "hollow" one. That is, there were great badger setts all round the place and it was impossible to stop all of them. He had frequently to make use of terriers in order to show sport. The terriers were not taken by a terrier-man as is the custom today. They ran with the hounds and if they got a bit behind they stuck to the line and were sure to come up with the pack when they were wanted. They were completely steady from riot so that, drawing with the pack and trying every earth they gave a fox a very poor chance of remaining unfound. Davies says that a squeak from a terrier was the sure signal of a find and there was not a hound in the pack that would not fly to it as eagerly as to Russell's horn or to his wild and marvellous scream. But this could have disadvantages. A fox might go to ground in a big and undiggable badger sett from which he could not be shifted; but the terriers would be there and would be to ground before they could be stopped. Also, it might be that they were a long way from the nearest farm or cottage where digging tools could be procured.

But, perhaps, the most telling point against terriers running with hounds is that a keen dog, in his eagerness to get forward could strain his heart and thus shorten his life. In fairness it must be said that there is no record of this happening to any of Russell's dogs.

Russell must have arranged for a certain amount of earth-stopping, but because his country was big, he must have found it difficult to deal with all the earths. It is known that he had a recipe for a compound which would keep a fox out of an earth and Will Rawle, his man, would stop earths and then sprinkle a few drops of this mixture on top. It probably contained asafoetida and if Rawle got it on his hands or his clothing he would stink like a polecat for days, as no amount of washing would dispel the horrible smell.

It is not known how Russell managed when he took his hounds to far distant meets, as he frequently did. It is improbable that he took the terriers on such long journeys. Perhaps he made use of local terriers.

After some ninety years, there can be none of the original Russell blood left today. Even if one could trace a terrier's pedigree back to Russell's dogs, there must have been so many outcrosses that the original blood would have been thinned to vanishing point. If one had bred true, one would now be producing half-wits. As an illustration of what in-breeding can do, the author remembers that in his youth, when there was little mechanised transport, every village had one or two "naturals", because the young men married girls from next door. Over a period of years, this in-breeding resulted in some children being born "simple". Nowadays, with the coming of the car and the motor-bike, the village boys can range farther afield for their brides with the result that the village "natural" is a thing of the past.

What is sometimes forgotten is that John Russell bred a *type* of fox-terrier, not a separate breed. Indeed, his terriers conformed to the Kennel Club specification. He gave up showing and judging as he considered that the show breeders did not prove their dogs' gameness and, to Russell, gameness was the important characteristic of a terrier. Although his favourites shared his fireside, they all worked to fox. One can imagine that any young dog that showed reluctance to face its enemy underground was speedily got rid of.

## VII

## ARTHUR HEINEMANN

After Russell's death, the next great name in the breeding of working terriers is that of Arthur Blake Heinemann who built up what was probably the best known kennel in the world. Although he was Sussex born, he spent most of his life on Exmoor. He was born in 1871 and was educated at Eton and Cambridge. There is a story that John Russell prepared him for Eton, but this must be regarded with dubiety.

After Cambridge he went to South Africa for a time and when he returned he got the idea that a quiet rectory on Exmoor would suit him and his sporting tastes, so he decided to enter the church, though a more unsuitable candidate it would have been hard to find.

He came to Porlock to study with Prebendary Hook and he lived in a little cottage in Hawkcombe called "Peep-Out". Even to the uncensorious people of Exmoor, Heinemann was a very rum candidate for the ministry. However, he regularly attended church with a large prayer-book under his arm.

His undoing came when he had to go away to a clergy retreat. Someone who saw him on the railway platform as he waited for the train said that he was wearing a curly-brimmed billycock hat and a long coaching overcoat with big pearl buttons. What was thought when this incongruous figure arrived at the retreat can be imagined.

He did not last long. On the second day everyone was

supposed to fast and, in the evening, the sound of hammering was heard from Heinemann's room. The Principal entered and found the hawk in his dovecote hammering away at a tin of bully beef which he had smuggled in. Heinemann's ecclesiastical career came to an abrupt end.

On an adequate private income, Heinemann continued to live at Peep-Out with several terriers, a tame badger and a tame otter. They all lived together on the best of terms. After his marriage he went to live at Bowling Green a short distance away. He also became Master of the old Essex Otterhounds, travelling between Essex and Devon for his sport. In 1902 he heard that Mr. William Cheriton who owned the Cheriton Otterhounds, wished to sell them. They hunted a big country in Devon. In Heinemann's own words: "I shall never forget my first visit to him. For hours he refused me a glimpse of the pack and kept assuring me that he would sell and was not asking an exorbitant figure, though he would not name the price, and all this muggy afternoon we were imbibing hot gin. Finally he fixed the price at £50 and showed me the pack. Most of them were too old and fat as puddings, but there were some good, rough hounds among them. I agreed to Mr. Cheriton's terms provided he circularised the water-owners in my favour, publicly acknowledged me as his successor, and kept the hounds until I wanted them. This he did loyally."

After a short time Heinemann resigned his Mastership of the Essex Otterhounds and gave his considerable talents to the Cheriton. And so began three years in which he showed unparalleled sport. He kennelled the hounds at Porlock during the winter and at the Braunton Road Repository during the hunting season.

He used to keep his hounds fit and sharp by letting them hunt his tame badger on Lucott Moor, giving the badger twenty minutes start. He also laid trails on Porlock marshes with his tame otter "Louie", always finishing up at a drain or culvert. At this time Heinemann had the unique experience of feeding three packs of hounds, exercising one and walking out with another, all in one day. They were the Exmoor Foxhounds, Peter Ormrod's Staghounds at Oare and then back with the latter to Porlock, where he kennelled them while he fed the Cheriton Otterhounds.

Heinemann had already built up the kennel of terriers which were to become so famous. He obtained his original stock from Squire Nicholas Snow of Oare who, in turn had obtained his from John Russell. His kennelmaid was Miss Annie Rawle, afterwards Mrs. Harris, who had been brought up with terriers as her grandfather and father were both great terrier men. They also had obtained terriers from Mr. Snow.

Here is Heinemann again: "Terriers, of which I held a strong hand, were not often really wanted in the Cheriton country, but one day I had no less than eight to ground together to an otter under an oak tree overhanging Hawkridge Wood Pool. Mirabile dictu! The terriers did not fight, but the otter dived through the air, without standing upon the order of his going, right over the shoulder of a Baron Von Sauerkraut, who was so pleased that he handed the secretary two guineas."

On another occasion, when he could see ahead and control them, Heinemann had five and half couple of terriers out. They drew well and helped hounds and were always picked up at the kill.

Twice, the terriers nearly caused a serious accident. The first time was when Heinemann was starting out for a ride with his hounds. They became excited and bayed his pony. The terriers pinned the animal by the hocks and both man and horse were nearly impaled on the railings at Porlock

A badger-digging party, photographed at Lynmouth, Devon in 1910. The bowler-hatted man with the pipe in the centre of the photograph is Arthur Heinemann.

(*Above*) A real "old-fashioned" sort is Gipsy who belongs to Mrs. Valerie Hoursell of Rushden, Northamptonshire. She was bred by Arthur Corby, the terrier man to the Oakley Hunt. (*Below*) Another broken-coated terrier, Sheena. She has won many cups as best of breed and supreme champion and still works to fox. Sheena is owned by Mrs. R. Curmore of Houghton-le-Spring, County Durham.

Church. Another time, the terriers attacked Heinemann's mare and hung on to her like leeches, and she gave him a very rough ride before he could throw himself off. This was at Oareford.

In 1905 Heinemann found that he could not carry on as Master of Otterhounds and sold the pack to Mr. W. Loraine Bell, Master of the East Galway Foxhounds, for £120. For three seasons he had shown wonderful sport and had bred a first-class pack of hounds.

Mrs. Harris was related to Will Rawle, John Russell's kennellman. She was of enormous help to Heinemann in the breeding and management of his terriers. He was a great badger-digger and in 1894 he founded the Devon and Somerset Badger Club, which was in being in the 1930s. The objects of the club were: the promotion of badger-digging and interest in badger-digging generally and also the breeding of working terriers. The name of the club was later changed to the Parson Jack Russell Club. After Heinemann's death in 1930, Mrs. Harris assumed the Mastership. She went as housekeeper to Mr. Henry Williamson, the famous Westcountry author and, some time after Heinemann's death, she produced a kitbag crammed with pedigrees, manuscripts and photographs which she hoped Mr. Williamson might use for a biography. He was unable to do so and it is not known what happened to the contents of the bag.

Like John Russell, Heinemann insisted that gameness was the first requisite in a terrier. He also insisted that his terriers were pure-bred to Russell's stock, and that he could trace their pedigrees back to 1890. He said that he never went outside the Westcountry for new blood. In his own words: "We are very much opposed to the modern show terrier and his type. Once you begin to breed it for show type, you lose the working qualities upon which you pride those terriers. I have been, I might say, the protagonist of the terrier bred for sport as against the terrier bred for show. I have no interest in cup hunting."

In addition to his hunting and his badger-digging, Heinemann was a gifted sporting journalist and contributed to most of the sporting journals of his day under the nom-de-plume of "Peep-Out". Although he disliked the show types, he judged at Cruft's on many occasions. He was a sociable, happy-go-lucky fellow, with very little money sense. I knew him well and recall that he was very kind to me on a number of occasions though he was a much older man.

I remember him best sitting in the ingle-nook of a village pub with a glass of whisky at his elbow and his short-stemmed, big-bowled pipe in his badger-scarred right hand, and being hail fellow well met with everyone.

Unfortunately, Heinemann's lack of money sense brought disaster. It is said that he went through £70,000 early in life and in middle age he was so poor that he was forced to go and live in a semi-detached farm labourer's cottage at Langley Marsh, near Wiveliscombe. He was broke to the wide in the 1920s but, fortunately, the late Tim Sedgwick, then assistant editor of *The Shooting Times*, heard of his plight and made him hunting editor of the paper. He had a weekly page in which he wrote about sport in the Westcountry and so was saved from absolute penury.

On New Year's Day, 1930, Arthur Heinemann went coursing. It was bitterly cold and, during the day, he fell into a pond. He did not go home until the coursing was ended and within a week he was dead from pneumonia. He was in his sixtieth year.

At this point I would like to pay tribute to Arthur Heinemann, a man who was so kind to a small boy and who gave that boy his first couple of terriers. Nothing was too much trouble and no question went unanswered. It is good to know that there are still terriers about which can be traced back to the Heinemann strain and that, so long as men love a game terrier, his name will be remembered.

After his death, the terriers were taken over by Mrs. Harris for the second time. The first had been during the 1914-18 war, when Heinemann was away in the forces. She very quickly took the place of Heinemann as the arbiter of the Russell type terriers and she carried on breeding the type of terrier which Heinemann had loved. In her heyday she had some 50 puppies out to walk each year. She sent her stock all over the world. Her method of breeding was to use only dogs and bitches of proved gameness. At the latter end of her life she went to live at North Molton and her kennel was dispersed, but there are still many dogs about which can be traced back to her breeding.

Another of the early breeders of Russell terriers was Miss Alys Serrell, author of *With Hound and Terrier in the Field.* Her father was a sporting parson and a friend of Russell's who gave him terriers. Miss Serrell had an excellent kennel of real workers — all smooth-coated. She was a tall, mannish woman who spoke with a lisp and extremely fast, which made her difficult to understand. In her book she says that she had hunted everything from rats to otters with her terriers; she had them under such control that, hard as they were, she needed only a handkerchief in her hand to keep them under restraint. Her foundation dog was "Redcap" born in 1890 of unknown ancestry. She says, "He had a beautiful bright tan head, with a black mark under the right ear, which was constantly transmitted to his descendants. His head was of medium length, without a trace of greyhound about it. His ears were small and well-carried, and his jaws long and punishing with big, strong teeth, and at eleven years of age he had lost only one small front tooth. His legs were straight and he had good feet, with a pad like leather. In size he was, I consider, perfect for underground work, his weight being 16 lb. He was short and compact everywhere, with the very best coat that could be — short, hard and dense — with plenty of undergrowth and thick skin."

Miss Serrell's bitch Amber was by a grandson of Russell's Tip. She was hard as nails and would face any watery drain. Once, she tackled a squeaky ploughshare and nearly broke her jaw. She weighed 16 lb., had a tan head and a hard, broken coat. She was so keen that anyone who held her back when work was in prospect, usually got bitten for his pains.

Another dog, Redstart, was the grandson of Redcap and Amber. Miss Serrell describes him as being so hard that one day when a cat crossed his path, he got hold of it and continued running till he threw it down dead. He was an utterly reckless dog and would tackle anything.

Miss Serrell entered her terriers to otter by taking a young otter on a long lead and running it along the river bank and into the water. She then encouraged the terriers to hunt the drag.

Like Russell, she had no success when she started hunting otter. The first time she took her terriers down to the River Lyd, she was disgusted that they started to fight when let out of the cart. She quickly stopped that and made peace but, apart from one dog being nearly drowned, nothing happened. She hunted otters until the end of 1892, when Mr. Courtenay Tracey brought his otterhounds down to hunt the river.

On reading her book, one can sense the enormous pride Miss Serrell had in her terriers. Like Russell and, later on, Heinemann, she was insistent on hardihood and gameness and she bred only from dogs which had proved themselves.

Miss Serrell's terriers were the foundation of the kennel of the late Miss Augusta Guest, daughter to Mr. Merthyr Guest who hunted the Blackmore Vale country with such munificence from 1884 to 1890. In 1913 Miss Guest started her own private pack of foxhounds and kept them on until 1953, when she became Joint-Master of the Blackmore Vale. She remained Joint-Master until her death in 1960. Before the 1939-45 war, she hunted hounds herself and only gave up riding when she was more than 70, when she took to a Landrover.

Miss Guest was devoted to her terriers and never docked them. In November 1956, she wrote to *Horse and Hound*: "I have a line of terriers distinctly tracing back to his (Russell's) by name, viz: Jack Russell's Ajax I and Ajax II and Old Tip, through Miss Alys Serrell's Redtop and my Rachel though, as that is practically seventeen generations back, I do not suppose the Jack Russell blood is still predominant. I can also trace back through my Pixie, the dam of which was said to be a Jack Russell dog, but I cannot vouch for that, it being so long ago. I have kept my pedigrees very carefully and have only gone for an outcross to a working strain, when necessary, that I can rely on." In June, 1957, Miss Guest wrote again saying that she did not know anyone who had kept the dogs pure and typical, but that the late Jack Cobby, huntsman of the South and West Wilts, had the only outcross that she used. She knew that his Russell terriers definitely had no show blood.

As has been said, Heinemann never went outside the Westcountry for new blood and never bred from a terrier which had not proved its gameness. One can trace the breeding of some of his terriers from the prefixes to their names. Stagshead Chloe, Lynton Jack, Williton Dapper, Bridgtown Bingo, Ellicombe Spot, Milton Zib, Porlock Vengeance and Vixen, Handycross Nestor and Pal were some of the names recorded by Heinemann. "Williton" was the prefix of a Mr. Notley who was a great badger-digger;

"Stagshead" terriers were the property of a keeper on the Baronsdown Estate, Dulverton; "Handycross" was Mrs. Harris's prefix before she took over the Heinemann terriers; "Milton" was the prefix of Phillip Everard, secretary of the Devon and Somerset Staghounds; "Ellicombe" meant that the dog had been bred by Will Rawle of Ellicombe, near Minehead; Lynton Jack went back to Mr. Nicholas Snow's terriers.

The people who have been mentioned were all Westcountry breeders of the Russell type of terrier and all of them worked their terriers. There are still dogs about today which can be traced back to their breeding.

## VIII

## THE PRESENT DAY

One sees them everywhere today; all sorts and conditions of terriers, and all of them called "Jack Russells" by their fond owners. Terriers of indeterminate ancestry, old-fashioned, working Sealyhams and little short-legged terriers have all come to be known as "Jack Russells".

The reason for this is that there has grown up a cult — and a snob cult at that — which makes the possession of a "Russell" terrier something of a status symbol. The tragedy is that so many of them are owned by townspeople and never have a chance to work. Indeed, their owners would disapprove of their working as they have no time or inclination for field sports or, if they are ladies, they cannot bear the thought of their dogs being bitten.

Now, these terriers are no doubt lovable and, very often, game little dogs, but they are not, repeat not, Jack Russells. The standard for a real Jack Russell terrier is that laid down by "Otter" Davies, and one should not budge from it. That is, the standard, given earlier in this book, of Trump, Jack Russell's first dog.

In *The Shooting Times* on September 15th, 1973 there appeared a report of a terrier show in which it was said that the Jack Russell classes gave the judges a major problem as the prevailing hunting terrain had led to the terriers being refined to a short-legged strain, falling a couple of inches short of the recognised standard.

There should have been no problem at all about this, as

those terriers were not Jack Russells. Surely, the sensible thing would be to call them what they are — working terriers, and to have a separate class for the real Russell types. This report went on to say that it would seem that a division of the class was required, though this, in its turn, would produce a query — should the breed be further sub-divided into rough and smooth divisions? What on earth would be the end if this were done? The Jack Russell terrier is not a breed, it is a type and why should there be sub-divisions? Either a terrier is a Russell or it is not. If you start dividing them up into large and small, you may well end up with miniatures as has happened with the poodle and look at the result of that! This talk of sub-divisions should be squashed immediately. Any terrier which does not come up to the Russell standard should be known simply as a working terrier. There is nothing derogatory in this. Most of them are game and nailers at a fox and it is hard to understand why the term "Jack Russell" should be such a cachet.

Even at an advanced age, I still have an eye and an admiration for the other sex, but it must be admitted that it is the ladies who are responsible for a lot of this nonsense. They know vaguely that a Jack Russell terrier is the "in" dog to have, but they want cuddly little animals and so the professional breeder falls in with their requirements. And who can blame him, as it is his living? But to the old-fashioned purist it is a sad state of affairs. As Russell terriers are not recognised as a separate breed by the Kennel Club, there is no breed register. The unofficial standard is that laid down by "Otter" Davies. Because of this it is very difficult to check pedigrees and any unscrupulous breeder can cobble a pedigree with little danger of being found out. Fortunately, these people are very few, but it can happen.

At the time of writing there is a strong movement to get Russell terriers recognised. The main support for this comes from breeders who get all or part of their living from their dogs. Now, if the terriers are recognised, they will be eligible to appear at Kennel Club shows and dogs which win in these shows become worth a great deal of money, so that their owners are very relucatant to work them in case they get scarred. As mentioned earlier, with Russell terriers, gameness and temperament are fully as important as make and shape and one cannot tell if a dog has the right temperament if he is not worked. Because he is a fighter does not mean that he will be game underground. Indeed, the gassy, yappy dog which sets up at every opportunity is very often a coward when he meets the right article. I mistrust a dog which carries his tail too gaily as I have found that a real worker nearly always carries his tail straight out, nearly parallel with the ground. Only when he is at work does the tail come up and wag.

By and large I think it would be a bad thing for the Russell type if it were recognised by the Kennel Club. We have seen what happens to other working breeds when the show people get hold of them and I, for one, should hate to think of it happening to the Russell. If these terriers ever become soft-bred show-dogs, John Russell will turn in his grave.

This must not be taken to mean that all show terriers are not game. Some of them are and very lovely dogs they are, as well. But the majority of them never have a chance to prove themselves. Even if one lives in a town it is good to know that one's terrier has come of the right sort of parents; although I, for one, think that no Russell should ever be condemned to live an urban life.

Oddly enough, it is in the north of England that one sees more of the true Russell type. The Fell and Moorland Working Terrier Club's shows have classes for the Russell and in them one can see the real article. All of these terriers work to fox, mostly in a rough and wild country which is far more demanding of a dog than the gentler countryside of the south. The aims of the club are fourfold: to rescue trapped terriers; to improve the strains of working terriers by retaining the old strains; to encourage working terrier shows; to try and provide a foster service if required. Any club members whose terrier is trapped underground contacts the nearest club representative for help and notifies the secretary. On receipt of a plea for help other members turn out and dig until the terrier is rescued or until it is found to be hopeless. The members of the club are all working men and it is wonderful to read the reports in the club's Year Book of the rescues which have been made. Men on night shift turn up during the day and those on day shift take over during the night and work goes on until the terrier is reached. Unfortunately, not all attempts are successful, but work is carried on until all hope of saving the dog is gone. The terriers used are mainly Russells, Borders and Lakelands.

Here are some extracts from the Year Book:

"On April 1st, 1970, a small Russell bitch named Peggy went to ground at 12.30 p.m. in a very large, loose ash-tip alongside an old railway siding. The terrier was baying for about an hour, then all went silent. The club's representative went to the spot at 4.30 p.m. They opened up the hole the terrier had entered to see the run of the hole, then about fifteen feet back a deep trench was dug and the hole was found about eight feet down. By the light of a torch it was seen to be blocked with loose ash. This was cleaned out and the terrier was found safe and alive with a live fox. The time was 10.30 p.m.

"On the 8th November, the same bitch was in trouble in a small sand hole. She had gone to ground at 2 p.m. Baying was heard for a short time, then all went quiet. The club's representative arrived at 5.30 p.m. The terrier could then be heard faintly. A trench was dug fifteen feet along the bank. This found the hole about six feet down and there was a small rabbit hole adjoining the main hole. The terrier was jammed in this and it was brought out safely at 8 p.m. The club's representative on each occasion was Mr. Neil Dewhurst.

"Mr. Dewhurst also reported that on Sunday, 27th December three terriers got badly stuck in a sand hole at the foot of a massive bank. He was told about this on the Tuesday and went to help. He found that the club members had dug about 20 feet into the bank, but the hole was only just big enough to crawl into. This was very dangerous. He decided to stay and they dug all night and enlarged the tunnel to about five feet square and shored it up with timber. They had gone about 25 feet into the bank and could hear the terriers. Other helpers then arrived. The tunnel was fairly sound in the roof and sides, as it was under a thick layer of hard marl and sandstone, but by late afternoon the rescuers met trouble. They were in about 30 feet and very near the terriers when they hit very loose, fine sand and the roof started to drop in small sections. Then, suddenly, the whole roof dropped in filling about ten feet of the tunnel, the sides of which had weakened. It was then decided that the only way the terriers could be saved was by a machine and a D6 Bulldozer was obtained. But when the firm's representative arrived he said the type of machine needed could not be used owing to the state of the ground. The only thing left was the tunnel so the diggers set to, to remove the loose sand. As they did so, more sand kept dropping in, but they kept it moving, hoping for a chance to get some props in. It was then 2 p.m. on the Wednesday. By Thursday the tunnel was nearly cleared, but the cavern in the loose sand was about twelve feet across by ten feet high and very dangerous. At this point, the whole of the far side of the cavern slipped, narrowly missing one of the diggers. When it settled, a hole had been exposed and from this the three terriers came out safe and sound. Mr. Dewhurst said that he was glad to come out of that hole as any terrier.

"From the Pennine Area, Mr. A. H. Lockwood reported that a fox was disturbed lying out on some crags. A Russell terrier, Prince, gave chase and, after about a hundred yards, they were seen to go to ground under a large rock. No sound was heard for a time, and it was then decided to put in another terrier, Tiny, with Candy, a Border terrier. Immediately they were put in they were heard to cry out as if in pain, unlike their usual baying upon meeting with fox or badger. No other sound was heard for about fifteen minutes and it was decided to investigate. Mr. Lockwood dropped down under the rocks and found a hole going into the hillside. He enlarged the entrance and shone a torch up it. On seeing what he thought to be a terrier, he crawled up and found Tiny dead. He dragged her out and went in again to find Candy also dead. He could see Prince farther up. He took Candy out and went in to get Prince. By this time he was gasping for breath which, he thought, was caused by his struggle to crawl up the hole, which was very tight.

"When Mr. Lockwood got to Prince the dog's head was thrust into a small hole. He got hold of his hindlegs and pulled him clear, but as he started to come out he felt his limbs become numb and it was difficult to breathe. Another man realising something was wrong, got hold of Mr. Lockwood's feet and pulled him out. Once in the open, Mr. Lockwood came to and found that they had been joined by a number of other men. He walked back to his car and felt worse and it was decided that he needed medical attention. He was helped into a van and passed out. When Mr. Lockwood came round he was in hospital wearing an oxygen mask and he was told that he was suffering from gas poisoning from black damp. He had lost three good terriers and nearly died himself."

This tragic, modestly-told story, shows how both terriers and men can get into trouble, though black damp is of a rare occurrence. There are plenty of other hazards, as the Year Book, again, illustrates:

"On Sunday, January 17th, 1971, a Russell terrier was being exercised on a hillside at Houghton-le-Spring. She disappeared. Her owner searched for her until three a.m. the following day. Late on the Monday afternoon, a party of helpers from the club was summoned and they searched until eleven p.m. without success. The search was resumed on the Tuesday and again a long search was made with no result. On the Wednesday the owner of the bitch found her to ground and freed her. She was unharmed.

"From the Durham area, Mr. J. Winch reported that on Sunday, January 10th, 1971 he was hunting foxes by request of local farmers and the Braes of Derwent Hunt. He was accompanied by his wife and Mr. Brian Johnson. He put his Lakeland terrier, Chanter, to ground at 11.30 a.m. and heard him no more. Mr. Johnson put in his Russell terrier Bryn as a finder at 2 p.m. and they began to dig to his baying. At 5.30 they realised that further help would be needed and four other members of the club arrived at 7 p.m. A tunnel was dug 16 feet into the side of the bank by lamplight. At midnight a tree fell down, bringing down the roof of the cavern and the Russell terrier fell from the roof. Digging for the Lakeland was continued until 2.30 a.m."

On the Monday they began again at 8 a.m. by felling a second tree and then dug on, but the terrier could not be heard. By noon digging was very difficult as, for every shovelful of sand taken off, two ran down and the diggers were in great danger. An excavator was summoned and digging went on until 10 p.m. without success. On the

Tuesday morning they began again at 8 a.m. By this time television reporters and cameras were present.

Digging by machine and hand labour enabled a gradual approach to be made to the terrier and at 6 p.m. the terrier was reached. He was in good condition and none the worse for his ordeal. Mr. Winch added to his report that celebrations were held at the Hat and Feather. Some of the men had sacrificed up to three day's wages and risked great danger to rescue this terrier.

These are only a few examples of the work done by the Fell and Moorland Working Terrier Club, a most deserving organisation. Many terriers which would otherwise have perished have been saved by these devoted men and the club is well worthy of support. The subscription, including a club badge is only 50p a year and one would like to see the club's activities spread over the whole country. Further information may be obtained from The Secretary, 48 Brownhill Road, Birstall, Batley, Yorkshire.

The northern moorland, the Fells and the Border country are wild and rugged with deep cracks in the rocks. It is mostly in these places that the terriers get trapped. In the south one seldom hears of terriers being lost for more than a few hours as the earth is diggable. It does happen on occasion, however, and it is then that skilled and willing help is vitally necessary.

It is as well to say here that one should never, repeat never, allow one's terrier to go to ground in a hunting country without the permission of the Master. Every Hunt has its own terrier man, either amateur or professional, and it is his job to see that the fox is dealt with in as humane and expeditious way as possible — that is, he is shot with a humane killer as soon as he is reached.

For those who have no knowledge of terrier work this is what happens. The hounds mark the fox to ground and the

Master calls for terriers with a distinctive call upon the horn. When the terriers arrive, hounds are taken some distance away. Now, it may be only a single hole or there might be a great many holes which form a network of tunnels. If it is desired to kill the fox, every hole except the one at which the hounds were scratching is blocked up with a spade. The terrier's collar is then taken off so that he will not get hung up on a projecting root, and he is loosed into the hole. It is a great mistake to cheer a dog on and it will make him so excited that he will throw his tongue when he is not up to the fox.

The terrier creeps into the earth and locates the fox in the dark by scent. If it is only a single hole, he will get up to his fox right away, but if there is a network of tunnels it may take him some time before he locates his enemy. When he does so and gets near to him the terrier should bay and keep on baying. If the fox has room he will retreat until he can go no farther and then the note of the terrier changes; it becomes urgent as though telling the men above that he is up to the fox. The terrier should not go right up to the fox, but should lie about two feet away from him and keep on baying. If the fox charges, the terrier should drive him back, but a really good terrier should never go in and make a fight of it. If he goes in and gets hold of the fox and it is a big place, one cannot hear him, but if he keeps baying the diggers know where he is. Again, the dog which goes in will spend a lot of his time in hospital as he will get bitten and a fox's bite is no joke. Sometimes it pays to follow the hole along, but in a big place a trench will be dug to hit off the hole. Guided by the terrier's baying the diggers work on until they come to the dog which is then pulled out and the fox is shot.

That is a rough idea of what is done but, of course, there are times when one gets into trouble by not being able to hear the dog in a big place, or when one comes upon a layer of hard shillet.

Perhaps the worst of all is soft sand which can fall in behind the dog, thus blocking him off from the diggers and obliterating all sound. The best thing in a sand earth is to push a long stick up the hole, so that if there is a fall-in the hole is not lost.

Terriers can be likened to Dr. Jekyll and Mr. Hyde. In the house they are almost soft and love the fireside but, always, the great idea is "let's go out and kill something". Out in the open they are never still. They are always working a hedge or sniffing at a rabbit-hole. That is, those of the real working sort whose sporting instincts have not been dulled by generations of breeding as pets.

The entering of a young dog to fox is a job which requires a deal of skill. It is no good taking a young dog out and expecting him to go to ground the first time. The best thing is to have him out on a lead and when hounds mark to ground, let him see the other dogs working. Thus, he becomes used to horses, hounds and noise. After he has been out a few times he will show great interest in what is going on underground. When he is really keen, he should be loosed when the fox has been shot and allowed to draw it out into the open. The next time, when one has got near to the fox, one should pull the old dog out and let the young dog see the fox mask on. He will then learn that a fox has got a sharp end. If he is allowed to get badly bitten at this time it may put him off for life or, if he is one of the dare-devil sort, it can easily make him too hard. I believe that a hard dog thinks that the fox he is to ground to is the same one which had bitten him before and so he makes a real fight of it.

Terriers vary in development, like human beings, but, in general, a dog should not be entered to fox until he is at least fifteen months old and has developed. A very young

*(Above)* Two of Mr. Jack Price's bitches working in a big place. "Who's going first? .... *(Below)* .... "It's somebody else's turn!" This terrier had been to ground for four hours just before this photograph was taken. He belongs to Mr. H. Telfer of Leadgate.

The author photographed with Sarah and Sykie.

terrier can be ruined if he is mauled by being allowed to go to ground too young.

There are not so many rats about now as there were, owing to the operations of pest officers. For terrier men this is a pity as ratting is an excellent way of introducing a puppy to vermin. After he has been bitten once or twice a pup will very quickly learn to kill with one bite. One of the best places to go ratting is down a stream or riverside. The dogs can then hunt their prey and also they learn not to be afraid of water. A steel-pointed stick or an iron prodder is a very useful thing as a rat can often be induced to bolt by a little judicious prodding along the line of the hole. I am taking it for granted that the pups have all been inoculated against hard pad, distemper and hepatitis. Rats are notorious carriers of "the yellows" and a dog can get it even by drinking water in which a rat has urinated. It is much better to be safe than sorry.

Wounds should be dealt with immediately. The old treatment used to be to put on green oils, which have a carbolic base and which cause the wound to smart. Nowadays there are antiseptic powders which are contained in a puffer and which can be sprayed direct onto the wound. These powders dry a wound up and heal it in a remarkably short time. They also stop any swelling of the muzzle if they are applied immediately. Another thing to remember is that a terrier which has been to ground for any time is always thirsty and will be grateful for a drink of water. There is far more to working a terrier than this, but it can only be learned from experience and not from a book.

With regard to the question of whether working terriers should live in the house or be kennelled outside, there are two schools of thought. Many people of wide experience hold that working dogs of any breed should live outside in a kennel as living in a house tends to make them soft. The others, of whom I am one, think that the proper place for one's dog or dogs is in the house. My terriers have always been house-dwellers and they have been out with hounds day after day throughout the wet and cold Exmoor winters and yet they have never been sick or sorry. My belief is that the more one's dog is with one the more he understands and can almost catch what is in one's mind.

It is generally accepted that the Russell terriers should be either broken-coated or rough. This is not entirely correct, as some of Parson Jack's dogs came smooth. These smooth-haired dogs have one great advantage over the others and that is that they keep themselves clean and seldom or never need a bath. On a wet day a rough dog will come out of an earth a ball of mud and the only thing to do is to bath him. By so doing one takes the essential oil out of the coat. This greasiness of the coat is nature's protection against wet so, if it is washed away with warm water, the dog has no weather protection at all and if taken out on a cold wet day he can easily get pneumonia. It is not length of coat that counts, it is density and, if a dog has a really dense coat, it can be as smooth as you like and weather will not hurt him, provided he is not bathed. I have always kept smooths and, although they have been out all day in the vilest weather, they have never been sick or sorry.

I remember the late Jack Lawrence, who retired after a lifetime of distinguished hunt service, one day bringing out a rough-haired dog, which I remarked to be very clean and spruce. He said that it had got very dirty a few days before and he had had to bath it. It was a wild and windy day with frequent scads of rain and the dog got wet through. The next time I saw Lawrence I asked after the dog and he told me that it had died and he put it down to exposure on that wild day.

One thing to be careful of with a true-bred terrier is that it does not go off on its own. Once a dog starts doing this you are almost bound to lose it sooner or later. The dog will find an earth and go to ground and, many times, it will get out all right, but the pitcher will go once too often to the well and eventually he will get stuck, either by scratching up earth behind him or by a fall of soft earth. And there he is. Unfortunately, a terrier in this predicament does not make a noise and, though one searches and listens at every earth one finds, it is nearly impossible to find out where he is. The only thing would be to take another dog with one and see if he can locate the truant. Of course, if the dog is not found, he will die a miserable death from starvation or asphyxiation.

The deadliest thing of all is the terrier who strikes up a friendship with another dog and they go off hunting together. The worst combination is a terrier and a gun-dog. If there are sheep about, two dogs can do the most terrible damage and there is only one remedy — the gun. Once two dogs start sloping off together the sternest measures must be taken to stop it at once.

This brings up the question of discipline. Now, a terrier is an excitable and volatile type and excitability on the part of its owner communicates itself to the dog. The great thing is to exert discipline on oneself — a difficult thing to do — and remain calm. Terriers are like children, they know exactly how far they can go. I have always found that fair discipline from puppyhood is the way to do it. If a young puppy does something wrong, he should immediately be rated with a sting in the voice. Catch him in the act and tell him exactly what you think of him. Then, put him in his basket and sit down and read the paper. In a few minutes he will come to you with wagging tail, but do not give in. Tell him to go back, that he is in disgrace and that you don't wish to speak to him. Keep this up for half an hour and he will remember it. If, after this he still persists in wrong-doing, catch him in the act and give him six of the best, rating him all the time. The best thing to use is a very thin, whippy switch which will sting, but do no damage. It is no good giving him a gentle pat with the hand and saying "naughty dog". Like a child, he will say to himself "silly old fool" and carry on sinning. One good hiding at the right time will, in most cases, show him who is boss and you'll never have to do it again, and you'll avoid a lot of trouble in later life.

## IX

# THE YOUNG ENTRY

If you buy a puppy, you should always ask to see the sire and
the dam. Sometimes it is not possible to see the sire, but you
should make sure that he is of the right conformation. If you
are able to pick your own pup from the litter, so much the
better. Don't be in a hurry, but sit yourself down and watch
the puppies. Dangle your handkerchief in front of them and
pick the one that comes up and takes hold of it. Some people
always pick the smallest one of the litter as they believe,
quite rightly, that it must have the right temperament to
have survived. Puppies are absolutely selfish and the bigger
ones will push their smaller brethren out of the way to get at
the teat. So the smallest pup must have a lot of determination
to have kept alive.

There is another old-fashioned way of picking a pup.
Take the bitch away from the litter and then take the pups
out of their bed and put them in a far corner. Then let the
bitch in and take the first pup she picks up to take back to
the bed. This is called "Bitch's Pick" and a lot of people
believe that she will always pick up the best pup first.

Far too many people sell off pups at the age of six or seven
weeks. This is too young. I would prefer a pup to stay with
the bitch until it is at least two months old. By that time she
has weaned it, but it still needs the care and attention that
only she can give it. Two months is a far more sensible age at
which to take the pup from the bitch.

People who have no experience are revolted to see a bitch

regurgitate when weaning pups. There is no need to be surprised by this. It is nature's way of ensuring that the food is already partly digested. It is quite natural and there is no need to be horrified.

A young pup needs four small meals a day up to three months of age when it should be reduced to three. These should consist of corn-flakes with milk, minced meat, a little cod liver oil with a calcium tablet once a day. At four months two meals should be enough, then, at nine months one meal should be sufficient with a biscuit at night. If one reduces the number of meals too early, the hungry puppies will bolt their food and their little stomachs will not be strong enough to cope with it and they will have digestive troubles. When they are teething they should be given an uncooked marrow bone to chew on. Never, under any circumstances, give any dog a cooked bone. The raw bone splinters can be digested, but cooked ones are too hard and can rip an intestine and cause internal bleeding which will kill a dog.

Most people prefer a dog pup, but there is a great deal to be said for a bitch. A dog can be wilful and strong-minded and independent; whereas, a bitch is more eager to please, is more biddable and is generally easier to control. There is an old saying that a bitch *can* be a nuisance for six weeks in the year, but a dog is a nuisance every damned day. This is putting it a bit strongly but, by and large, there is a deal of truth in it.

Bitches should not be bred from until at least the second heat. I have found it best to wait until the thirteenth day before mating them. They are then fully ready and will stand for the dog. Terriers seldom have any trouble in whelping and are best left alone with only an occasional inspection to see that all is well.

There is, at the moment, a movement against the docking

of tails. The only reason for docking is to improve a terrier's appearance. Two thirds of the tail should be left on to afford a hand-grip in later life. If the docking is done at four days old, I am sure that the pups feel little. A pair of secateurs is the best thing to use. A quick snip, a dab of disinfectant and the job is done and the pup shows no sign of discomfort.

Most people take off dew-claws at the same time as they dock. Dew claws are the claws above the foot and people say they serve no useful purpose and can be a nuisance in later life. I have never taken dew claws off and I believe they do serve a useful purpose. Many a time I have watched a dog grooming himself and he uses the dew claws. If they are kept short and snipped above the quick now and again, I have never known them to cause trouble.

Most puppies are born with round worms and should be treated for this at six weeks of age. There are several proprietary products which are effective. They should then be dosed again at three months and at every three months after that. Grown dogs usually suffer from tapeworm which require a different sort of tablet. If pups, or indeed, grown dogs, suffer from diarrhoea, a simple remedy is a little arrowroot in milk. This should stop it.

Some litters of pups turn out to be fighters very early in life. Indeed, some of them have to be separated when eight weeks old. If they do this, never leave three together or two will turn upon the other, and kill it.

With grown dogs, if two bitches take a dislike to each other, you will never stop them fighting; the only thing to do is to get rid of one of them. There is no need to be alarmed if two fighting dogs make a lot of noise; they are not hurting each other seriously. The time to get worried is when they go quiet as this means that they are really in holds. You need two people to separate them. One should hold the dog which is being bitten by the tail and the scruff; the other person should put his hands round the biter's throat and with his thumbs force the tongue up. This will make him let go in nine cases out of ten. Care should be taken when the dogs are separated that they are firmly held or in the heat of the moment someone may get bitten.

It may be noticed that a grown puppy or an elder dog is scratching his ear continually. This should be dealt with at once as it is a sign of canker and if it is not attended to the dog will suffer a great deal of discomfort. There are a number of canker cures on the market, but the simplest, and in my opinion, the best, is the one made up from the recipe of the late Dick Sharpe who was; for many years, the Kennel-Editor of *The Shooting Times* and *Country Magazine*. It was printed so often in the magazine that it became known as the Shooting Times Canker Cure. Here is the recipe: one ounce of boracic powder, one ounce of zinc powder, one drachm of iodoform. Keep in a tightly corked bottle and put one saltspoonful in the ear each day. Massage the powder down to the base of the ear and repeat until cured. I have never known this to fail.

Working dogs can easily pick up ticks; these usually adhere round the ears and the neck. The treatment is to dab with petrol or paraffin and then seize the tick between the nails of forefinger and thumb and jerk it off with a quick twist. If the head is left in it will cause a bad sore. Mrs. Elsie Williams, author of *The Popular Fox Terrier* says that for lice, and fleas, she uses a mixture of equal parts of paraffin oil and warm cow's milk. It is applied with a toothbrush, and the afflicted part is then washed with warm water and thoroughly dried. She says that this mixture works like magic on all skin pests.

If a dog is off colour and refuses food do not attempt to force him to eat. Pick up his bowl immediately. He knows best what is good for him. If his refusal of food persists the next day, take him to the vet.

It is well worth while finding a good dog vet in the district. All veterinary surgeons have their strong points, with some it is cattle, with some horses, while others specialise in small animals. A good dog vet in whom one has confidence is a great morale booster when one's dog is ill. If in doubt, do not hesitate to go to him.

## X

## TERRIER SHOWS

It is only during the last few years that working terrier shows have become popular, but so great is the interest in them that they are now held all over the country. Usually, they are held in aid of the local hunt, although the Fell and Moorland Working Terrier Club holds shows in aid of club funds. Such shows are not to be regarded as life or death competitions but rather, as very pleasant country occasions where one meets other terrier people and sees all sorts of terriers. Usually there will be a championship cup for the best terrier and, in the bigger shows, a cup for the best dog and for the best bitch, together with cups for the winners of the various classes. The cups are nearly always "perpetual" ones which means that the winners hold them for a year and return them in time for the next show.

Shows vary in the number of classes held, but there are generally about eleven or twelve, such as: smooth dog, smooth bitch, puppy under six months, young dog or bitch between six and twelve months, rough dog, rough bitch, Border, Lakeland or Fell type terriers, veterans over eight years, Jack Russell type terriers, and so on.

Some shows have special classes for dogs with working certificates. These are given by a Master of Foxhounds and the wording is: "I certify that Mr. Blank's smooth-coated, tan and white fox-terrier dog (or bitch) Nettle, is a game terrier and has worked with the Blankshire Foxhounds. (Signed) A. N. Other, M. F. H. Blankshire Foxhounds." Of course, these classes, must, of necessity, be entered by dogs whose owners have the chance to work them. The fact that they will kill rats is of no use. For a working certificate they must be game to fox and the only person who can issue such a certificate is a Master of Foxhounds.

However, it doesn't matter if one has not got such a certificate. There are still lots of classes in which a terrier can be entered. Entries are taken on the field and the fee is about fifteen pence per entry. The person taking entries will tell you in which class your dog should be entered.

There is no need for a lot of grooming as there is in Kennel Club shows. These are working terrier shows and the judges are not looking for spruced-up dogs. A friend of mine took his dog out cubhunting one morning, it was to ground for some time and came out covered in dirt and with a bite on its nose. That afternoon he took it to a terrier show and carried off the championship, although the dog was still looking as though it had been shaken up in a bag of sand. In spite of the dirt, the dog was beautifully made and looked a real workman.

When the dogs are in the ring, there is no pushing them into position or holding up of the tails. The dogs are allowed to show themselves quite naturally. After all, any judge, if he is worthy of the name, can see what a dog is without the handler pulling the dog about. It is advisable to keep the dog on a short lead, as if he gets too near another dog it may result in a fight. It is also advisable, if the dog has been taken by car, to let him have a run as it is very embarrassing to have a dog cock his leg or empty himself when in the ring.

When the class is in the ring, they walk round so that the judges can have a good look at them. Then they are halted and each dog is individually examined.

The judges then return to the centre of the ring and call out the five or six they like the best. From these the first, second and third are chosen. The prize-winners all receive rosettes.

From going to these shows one gets a very good idea of what a working terrier should be. But, as there is no general standard laid down, judges vary in their preferences. Some like terriers with a bit of daylight under them, while others like the short-legged variety. One will notice that a terrier which is in the money at one show can be out of the running at another with different judges.

The Jack Russell, as do all classes, have a standard, but one certainly sees some queer-looking objects masquerading under that title. If one was a purist and took the thing too seriously, one would turn down every terrier that was docked, but that would mean that very few of them would be eligible.

One thing to remember is never to criticise the judging. One may disagree strongly with the judges' verdict, but it must be accepted in a good spirit. Judging is not an easy job and they are there to be shot at. It is not too much to say that the way to make enemies is to judge at any sort of show. This is by no means to say that the pot-hunters have crept in. They take their good-looking terriers round the shows and if they do not win they are quite capable of going up to a judge and telling him he knows nothing about terriers. I remember one gentleman coming up to me before a show and telling me that his dog had won several championships. I told him he had no business to tell me that and I called the ring steward and said that I refused to judge the terrier. He was given his money back and I had made an enemy for life.

On one occasion a friend of mine, who is an outstanding judge, was officiating at a big show. The choice for the championship lay finally between two dogs. The judge knew that one was a worker, but he was doubtful about the other. At the side of the field was a long, thick hedgerow. "Come with me", said he and left the ring. The dog did not know what to do. It came to a cigarette packet and played with it and clearly showed that it had never been worked. The judge then turned to the other and told him to let his dog work the hedge. The dog which did not know its job was beautiful on conformation and looks, but the championship went to the other. After all it was a *working* terrier show.

It is a great pity that this pot-hunting has reared its ugly head. It is, one supposes, inevitable, but it leaves a very nasty taste behind it. The verdict of the judges should always be cheerfully accepted.

In these working terrier shows there are usually two judges, a Hunt Servant and knowledgable amateur. They receive no fee and have often come a long way to judge so that it is all the more important that their verdicts should be accepted with good grace.

In conjunction with terrier shows, terrier racing is often held and there is no more amusing sight than a pack of terriers racing after a fox's brush. The races are usually run in heats of six and a final. The terriers are confined in traps which open simultaneously. A fox's brush is attached to an endless wire which goes round the back wheel of a Landrover. The brush is dangled in front of the traps and the dogs go mad. There is a frenzied outburst of barking and then the traps go up. Off they go after the brush which the driver of the Landrover tries to keep just in front of them. Sometimes he doesn't succeed and the terriers get the brush and then start a melee with the owners diving in to pull out their dogs. It is always advisable to have someone waiting at the end of the track to pick up the dog as soon as they pass the winning post.

Sometimes, to add variety, there is a steeplechase course with hay bales placed at intervals across the track. It is a most comical sight when the shorter-legged dogs scramble over the bales, yelping in their anxiety to get forward.

Terrier racing is a great added attraction to any show.

It should not be assumed that because they are called working terriers shows, dogs which have not been worked are barred. Any terriers are welcome and are sure to find a class to suit them. Their owners will have a very pleasant afternoon out and, if they receive a rosette, they will go home singing.

One final word. Always remember that your dog is probably the truest friend you will find in this wicked world. He doesn't criticise and he bears no malice. You are, or should be, the end all and the be all of his existence, so it is up to you to look after him. Working terriers are all too often the unsung heroes of the world; they don't ask much — food, a comfortable place to sleep and exercise, with the chance of a bit of hunting now and then. In return they give you their complete devotion.

"And, on the Last Day, O Little One, thou shalt wag a Tiny Tail of Gold" Martin Luther.

# ACKNOWLEDGEMENTS

I owe thanks to so many people for their help in compiling this book. I am grateful to all those kind people who sent me photographs; they are too numerous to mention individually, so I hope that a blanket "thank you" will suffice.

Mr. J. R. C. Moore-Stevens has encouraged me by reading and commenting upon my manuscript.

The Fell and Moorland Working Terrier Club have been good enough to allow me to include extracts from their Year Book.

The staff of the Somerset County Library have been unfailing in getting reference books for me.

Mr. David Ridgway has been a great help with photography; finally, without the constant cajoling and bullying of my wife this book would never have been finished.

# BIBLIOGRAPHY

*Exmoor Memories*, A. G. Bradley.

*Hunting Parson*, Mrs. Eleanor Kerr, (1963).

*A Memoir of the Rev. John Russell*, E. W. L. Davies, (1882).

*The Sporting Magazine*, (1829).

*Exeter Gazette.*

*Bailey's Magazine.* (1874), (1885).

*Dogs of Britain*, Clifford.

*The Fox Terrier*, Rawdon Lee, (1890).

*The Dog*, "Stonehenge", (1872).

*With Hound and Terrier in the Field*, Alys Serrell.

*Horse and Hound*, (1956).

*The Shooting Times*, (1973).

*The Fell and Moorland Working Terrier Club Year Book*, (1970).

*Country Magazine.*

*The Popular Fox Terrier*, Mrs. Elsie Williams, (1965).

*All About the Jack Russell Terrier*, Mona Huxham, (1975).

*The Terrier's Vocation*, Geoffrey Sparrow, (1976).

# INDEX